Law, Human Creativity and Generative Artificial Intelligence

This book addresses the complex issue of human creativity in the age of Artificial Intelligence (AI).

AI is increasingly being used to create texts, images, and musical compositions. This increase in the application of AI within the creative industries can of course enhance human performance while producing creative and commercial challenges for human authors. Against this background, this book considers how current mechanisms for incentivising creativity – including legal regulations, such as copyright, state funding, and tax regimes – are inadequate in the age of AI. After acknowledging the opportunity that AI presents, the book then proposes alternative regulatory mechanisms through which human creativity can be incentivised.

This book will appeal to scholars and researchers in the areas of socio-legal studies, intellectual property law, media law, and law and technology.

Julija Kalpokienė is a Junior Research Fellow and teaches courses in Technology Law, Intellectual Property and AI in the Faculty of Law at Vytautas Magnus University, Lithuania.

Law, Human Creativity and Generative Artificial Intelligence

Regulatory Options

Julija Kalpokienė

Routledge
Taylor & Francis Group
a GlassHouse Book

First published 2024
by Routledge
4 Park Square, Milton Park, Abingdon, Oxon OX14 4RN

and by Routledge
605 Third Avenue, New York, NY 10158

Routledge is an imprint of the Taylor & Francis Group, an informa business

A GlassHouse book

© 2024 Julija Kalpokienė

British Library Cataloguing-in-Publication Data
A catalogue record for this book is available from the British Library

Library of Congress Cataloging-in-Publication Data
Names: Kalpokienė, Julija, author.
Title: Law, human creativity, and generative artificial intelligence : regulatory
    options / Julija Kalpokienė.
Description: Abingdon, Oxon [UK] ; New York, NY : Routledge, 2024. |
    Includes bibliographical references and index.
Identifiers: LCCN 2024015394 (print) | LCCN 2024015395 (ebook) |
    ISBN 9781032735870 (hardback) | ISBN 9781032735894 (paperback) |
    ISBN 9781003464976 (ebook)
Subjects: LCSH: Artificial intelligence—Law and legislation. | Creative ability.
Classification: LCC K564.C6 K35 2024 (print) | LCC K564.C6 (ebook) |
    DDC 343.09/998—dc23/eng/20240409
LC record available at https://lccn.loc.gov/2024015394
LC ebook record available at https://lccn.loc.gov/2024015395

ISBN: 978-1-032-73587-0 (hbk)
ISBN: 978-1-032-73589-4 (pbk)
ISBN: 978-1-003-46497-6 (ebk)

DOI: 10.4324/9781003464976

Typeset in Times New Roman
by Apex CoVantage, LLC

To my mother and late grandmother for being inspirational human authors and to my family – Ignas, Klemensas, Frederikas, Rachelė, and Samuelis – for their unwavering support.

Contents

1 Introduction

As generative AI systems increase in their sophistication, disruption of the art and creative product markets is a likely outcome, particularly due to the scale and cost efficiencies that these tools offer, which exposes human authors to substitution effects and thereby poses a threat to their income and necessitates a search for new and equitable remuneration options (Senftleben, 2023). As Sætra (2023, p. 3) warns, there is a strong likelihood that 'AI will . . . take content produced by humans, make it their own, and make the original creators obsolete'. However, opinions differ as to the effects of such substitution. Under the more progressivist approaches, for example, '[g]enerative AI training is essential for human beings to explore new avenues of artistic expression that are still unknown', particularly as the outputs of such machinic processes are seen to hold the potential to contribute to 'new forms of art and cultural expressions that benefit the society at large' (Geiger & Iaia, 2024, p. 7). Likewise, there is a rush to think of strategies to 'integrate these technologies into our current social structures and organisations to the benefit of society as a whole' instead of engaging in long-term threat mitigation (Tredinnick & Laybats, 2023, p. 47). This book, however, goes in a different direction: while acknowledging that the increasing encroachment of technologies on various domains of human life, including art, is going to continue and likely even accelerate, if not due to normative considerations, as in the earlier discussion, then due to market pressures, the core argument is that diverse human artist remuneration options need to be explored precisely in order to mitigate the potential threat of humans losing the material incentives to engage in creative activities.

Another development to note is both a quantitative and a qualitative increase in training data as a result of today's increasingly digital-first life, which means that new troves of training data are opened up: after all, 'the more data one can feed machine learners, the more and the better the programs one can grow' (see, e.g., Drott, 2021, p. 191). Moreover, such ample data and its automated analytics create opportunities for instant personalisation and tailoring of the offering to a particular user's taste, moods, etc. (Drott, 2021, p. 193; see also Morreale, 2021). However, even abundant data cannot

DOI: 10.4324/9781003464976-1

be used, especially for complex applications, without significant investment. Nevertheless, investment does require a return, kickstarting the search for ways to monetise both the technology itself and its output, thereby challenging traditional operational practices within artistic creation and the creative industries (Drott, 2021). In particular, human artists are threatened by generative AI's potential conjunction with platformisation: here, platform companies (such as streaming platforms) not only can access large troves of user data but also can 'replac[e] a one-time exchange with a durable relation of dependency' through subscription (Drott, 2021, p. 196; see also Morreale, 2021). Through subscription fees, platforms can lock users in through sunken costs *and* acquire a revenue stream that could make generative AI output profitable even without it being protectable. Hence, even if single AI-generated content items were monetarily worth little (if anything at all), as a package and service, they would still be able to generate profit to the detriment of human authors who may end up crowded out of such a service offering.

To some extent, it must be admitted that 'despite centuries of technological disruption, we do not live in a world of massive unemployment' since old jobs are being replaced by new ones across different sectors, including the arts (Hertzmann, 2018, p. 14). The common argument often put forward by proponents of AI across different sectors is that greater automation contributes to the public good by freeing up time otherwise devoted to low-status, low-income tasks and allowing individuals to concentrate on things that really matter (see, characteristically, Hertzmann, 2018, p. 15). Transposed into the artistic domain, this would mean the automation of mass-market creative works (such as background music, generic paintings such as those used for hotel interiors or sold to tourists, etc.). However, this would also mean taking away the ability to earn money on the side for young (and even established) artists while they are in the process of aspiring to the higher end of the market: as Drott (2021, p. 205) quips, '[l]iberation from mundane, menial tasks in these circumstances is tantamount to liberation from the ability to make a living' and from a creative economy as such. Moreover, since in the process of artistic creation it is hardly, if at all, possible to separate the drudgery from the actual output, the domain-wide effects are going to be particularly notable.

In particular, competition is to be felt by human artists on the lower levels of creative labour's pecking order, but as technology progresses, ever larger swathes of the arts and creative industries sector will be affected (Lee, 2022, p. 606). Indeed, although the effects of generative AI may be less tangible for high-profile established artists who can already rely on their status, less famous and up-and-coming artists would very likely find their opportunities significantly curtailed (Munden, 2022). Like in the Industrial Revolution that meant a shift from skilled artisans making their products to a mass unskilled (or low-skilled) workforce toiling in factories making mass-produced artefacts, generative AI might lead to a shift from artists creating their works to the mass-production of machine-generated content that, at least functionally, can pass as art (Newton & Dhole, 2023). Some argue that financial incentives are not justified and that artists tend to create for a broad variety of reasons, deriving incentives from diverse rewards, including the sheer satisfaction of partaking in the creative process or an altruistic drive to increase the societal good (see, e.g., Boyle, 2003). Nevertheless, from the regulatory standpoint, the provision and maintenance of monetary incentives tend to be at the heart of the matter, particularly because it is extremely difficult, if possible at all, to regulate through the law matters such as self-realisation or altruistic satisfaction. For this reason and given the changing structure of material incentives, the remuneration aspect is at the heart of this book.

Such search for incentivisation options admittedly goes against the grain in the sense that although creativity and innovation have been traditionally considered to be uniquely human qualities that are relatively immune to automation, generative AI is already threatening to upend and beginning to 'significantly alter creative work, both independent and salaried' (De Cremer, Bianzino and Falk, 2023). As such, three future scenarios are likely, as outlined by De Cremer, Bianzino, and Falk (2023): an explosion of creativity through AI's assistance, monopolisation of creativity by AI, or the coexistence of AI and human-generated content, with human-created works commanding a premium. All three themes, in various combinations, also play out in this book as they are not seen as mutually exclusive. The explosion of the amount of content enabled or completely generated by AI is already becoming evident, with it likely to become the dominant form of content generation. The question, then, is how to design regulations that provide for productive coexistence between human authors and AI content generators so that human-created works continue to have a viable niche in the market.

It is, of course, a long-standing problem that although a minority of artists enjoy tangible success and can live off the results of their labour, the majority languish at the tail-end of the popularity curve – a situation only exacerbated by streaming platforms that, while promising to increase discoverability, have in fact only expanded the pool of those vying for attention (Morreale, 2021, p. 107; Lee, 2022, p. 603). Hence, the size of the 'surplus artistic population' (i.e., those unable to generate sufficient economic incentives for their creative labour) has a tendency to increase with every innovation that expands the supply or artistic output (Morreale, 2021). Moreover, we are already inundated with content, artistic and otherwise, which means that audiences have insufficient time not only to consume but also, first and foremost, to even notice competing offerings. In this context, getting through the informational noise and overcoming the flood of competing offerings are particularly complex tasks. In fact, in the contemporary attention economy, the object of attention (which includes both human and artificial artists and their output) becomes less important than the very fact of attention attraction (Morreale, 2021,

p. 107). Artistic considerations, aesthetic value, and other features tradition-ally associated with the artistic domain could then be seen as becoming of secondary importance.

However, to better understand the further complexities brought about by generative AI, a discussion of the technological and theoretical contexts is merited. Beginning with the technologically enabled aspect, generative art can be defined as 'art that is generated wholly or at least in part by algo-rithms, and not by the direct control of the programmer or the programmer's customer', which is sometimes under direct human supervision but, at least in more complex cases, with significant autonomy delegated to AI in terms of making decisions about the content to be generated (Murray, 2023, p. 32). Such a lack of foreseeability and the consequent breaking of the causal link between humans and an ostensibly creative output can be seen as transforma-tional, not only complicating the status of AI-generated content (e.g., regard-ing copyright law) but also leaving plentiful unanswered questions as to the future role and standing of human authors as such (see generally Bonadio & McDonagh, 2020). Indeed, to an ever-larger degree, 'vital creative deci-sions are not made by humans, rather they are the expression of a computer learning by itself based on a set of parameters pre-defined by programmers' (Guadamuz, 2021, p. 148). Moreover, one could claim that current AI models go even further and largely avoid the need for pre-set parameters and instead ever more fully rely on machine learning. At the very least, therefore, there is an increased ambiguity as to the tripartite relationship among humans, machines, and creativity that perhaps even points towards a degree of conver-gence between humans and AI in the domain of creativity (Benedikter, 2021).

By being significantly more efficient (i.e., capable of producing more out-put in less time than humans could), generative AI poses a threat to the liveli-hoods of human artists, including, but not limited to, writers, visual artists, composers, filmmakers, etc.; the threat is only going to be increased by the fact that, once the initial investment has been made, the costs of running an AI tool are very low in contrast to hiring humans who need to be continuously remunerated for their creative endeavours (Naqvi, 2020, p. 28). The question of incentive and reward is crucial. Humans have a choice over their activi-ties and therefore need incentives to engage in one (e.g., creativity) over oth-ers, whereas AI tools lack such independent agency and thus do not need an incentive to create; hence, a cost-benefit consideration is set up whereby, once deployed, generative AI systems are significantly cheaper but simultane-ously raise questions as to whether their output necessitates the same or even a similar level of protection as the results of human creativity require (Picht & Thouvenin, 2023). After all, humans have to be rewarded for their choices, whereas machines, lacking such a choice, are seen as not meriting (and, no less importantly, unable to appreciate) such a reward. Nevertheless, acknowl-edgment of AI creativity tends to quasi-automatically invoke a competitive relationship between technology and human artists, even if this is not always merited (Wingström et al., 2022). However, as shown in this book, detrimental effects on human authors can occur even independently of AI's creative capacity, under whatever definition of the latter.

Still, part and parcel of the matter is that, as Shtefan (2021, p. 721) notes, '[t]here is no legal definition of creativity'. One could, in fact, debate whether such a definition is at all possible given the 'essentially contested nature' of the matter (Bown, 2021, p. 46). Notably, creativity as such is a term often seen as wrought with arbitrariness, which can only be (temporarily) suspended by legislative means: to quote an observation by Henriksen et al. (2022, p. 466), '[a]ssigning a definition to creativity, or deeming something creative, is often a political choice'. However, typically, creativity is understood as 'almost a mystified process that is tightly linked to properties such as corporeality, soul, emotions, insight, history, pain, suffering, etc.' (Millet et al., 2023, p. 2). Similarly, Tubadji et al. (2021) emphasise not only AI's inability to emotionally relate to its surroundings and its audiences but also its lack of both moral awareness and a value-based capacity of judgement. Paquette (2021, pp. 201–202) defines authorship or creatorship of a work as 'an elusive primordial concept that is unique to the human experience and originates from the conscious mind of man'. In general, however, one may expect creativity to manifest itself when 'a person reflects or transforms reality and expresses it in a specific objective form in their own way, making their own choice going beyond existing works, without repeating what was previously done by this or another person' (Shtefan, 2021, pp. 726–727). In terms of human versus machine creativity, the debate is therefore often cast as one referring to the results of 'the mysterious ingenuity of the human mind' versus mere simulation (Paquette, 2021, pp. 213–214).

Likewise, for Boden (2016, p. 67), creativity, which is understood as 'the ability to produce ideas or artefacts that are new, surprising, and valuable', can be seen as 'the acme of human intelligence'. Such definitions of creativity tend to rest on some version of innovativeness or groundbreaking novelty (see, e.g., Boden 2012). This, it will become evident, contrasts with, for example, actual practice, where for copyright, the innovativeness threshold can be rather low. Moreover, such an idealised take on creativity ignores that by far, not all human artists produce truly groundbreaking works regularly – or at all – thus leaving little substantial difference between human and AI creations, at least from a user perspective (Lee, 2022, p. 605). Meanwhile, other authors, despite going in a similar direction, are less ambitious and demanding. For example, the determination of whether creativity inheres in a particular AI model or not is seen to rest on whether it can 'produce solutions that are not replications of previous solutions that the AI system knows' and whether such solutions are task-appropriate (Ramalho, 2022, p. 18). For Poltronieri (2022, p. 31), creativity can be conceptualised as something that creates 'unique recombinations of existing elements, giving rise to new semantics in a process that expands our previously structured set of beliefs'. Nevertheless, the prevailing sentiment is still that of art being, fundamentally, an 'expression of human free will' that, as of now, cannot be emulated by machines – instead, the argument goes, anything generated by a machine 'will always be traceable back to a human desire to create' (Du Sautoy, 2020, p. 105). Hence, any innovation would always ultimately be traceable to a human. This is due to AI being unable to determine its own preferences and therefore remaining dependent upon human input (Spindler, 2022, p. 258). The preceding is also seen to extend beyond mere motivation and emotional capacity into more general qualities, such as embeddedness in a particular culture and within a specific context (Bisoyi, 2022, p. 382). Here, Potts (2023, pp. 154–155) offers an illustrative distinction between AI-generated and AI-authored content: generation involves a relatively low threshold and is associated more with mechanical production, whereas creativity necessitates the emulation of quasi-human capacities.

The work of art itself tends to be seen as revealing something specific about human nature and the essence of being human, almost causing in itself a number of unconcealments (see, e.g., Du Sautoy, 2020, pp. 2–3). However, there is also a flip side to such an argument as it immediately discards as essentially non-art everything that the perceiving individual fails to recognise as providing such an unconcealment, thereby paving the way to cultural biases – it is unsurprising that when examples are provided to illustrate this argument, they almost without exception come from the cannon of Western art (see Du Sautoy, 2020, pp. 2–3). Naturally, then, others tend to flip the preceding argument on its head and claim that creativity and, by extension, art-ness, lie not necessarily in the work itself but in their relational aspect vis-à-vis the audience, that is, in the projection of art-ness onto the work (see, e.g., Natale, 2022). Nevertheless, this view can also give rise to two radically different interpretations regarding AI-generated content. For Hertzmann (2018), for example, the social nature of art implies that there cannot be such a thing as machinic art proper as machines cannot interact with the broader social and cultural milieu. Nevertheless, AI does not learn and operate in a vacuum: on the contrary, as Arriagada (2020, p. 403) stresses, it is 'fundamentally based on Big Data, which is the most social thing we have since it shows patterns of social behaviour'. Meeting both interpretations mid-way, both creativity and the aesthetic experience of AI's results can be seen to reside in the collaboration between the artist and the AI model and are enacted through another collaborative relationship, this time with an audience (DiBlasi, 2022, p. 256; see also Audry & Ippolito, 2019).

It must be kept in mind that the dominant Western views on creativity 'are imbued with assumed beliefs, particularly around the individualist, humanist, positivist, and psychological ways of understanding creativity' that place the output of the human mind above everything else, all in the Cartesian tradition of mind-body dualism (Henriksen et al., 2022, p. 466). Such dualistic thinking extends beyond the opposition of mind and body towards that of human and non-human, always clearly prioritising the first element of such opposition, thereby rendering creativity (especially that performed in the Western tradition) as a specifically human faculty (Henriksen et al., 2022, p. 468). Clearly, such human-centrism is predicated upon the allegedly uniquely human qualities of 'reason, autonomy, impartiality, and universality' that, in turn, seemingly legitimise 'mastery, stewardship, and/or management of non-humans who are considered to lack these capabilities', with the latter entities and objects being relegated to a status that is merely instrumental (Mellamphy, 2021, p. 13). The human is thus posited as 'a creator of culture and technologies, bearer of rights and responsibilities, and a cultivating force that forges civilizations and political societies', who makes use of those that are seen as less worthy (Mellamphy, 2021, p. 14). This strong separation between humans and the rest ultimately means that when, contrary to expectations, 'artificial entities instantiate behaviors and activities that are typical of creative agents', their performance 'is perceived as dishonest or, even more drastically, it triggers uncomfortable feelings of rejection and discontent against the entities in question' (Moruzzi, 2020, p. 96). Seen in this light, it is not difficult to understand why some authors assert that the spread and adoption of generative AI capacities ultimately devalue creative practices (see, e.g., Eisikovits & Stubbs, 2023).

Similarly, Stephensen (2022) criticises the attempts to come up with a single universal definition of creativity as if it was a timeless and objective phenomenon that occurs identically across all cultures; instead, the idea of creativity is best seen as one invented (and potentially re-invented) under specific historical, cultural, and political circumstances – a realisation which then opens 'creativity' for further questioning, namely, *how* and *why* it has been invented and defined in the way that we understand it today. Perhaps even more fundamentally, however, the combination of an exalted status of creativity and AI encroaching on it 'can erode humans' ontological security about their unique position in the world' (Millet et al., 2023, pp. 1–2). Indeed, should AI, which lacks most, if not all, qualities and attributes typically considered to be human, be nevertheless admitted to possessing creative capacities, this admission 'might be phenomenologically equivalent to the experience of the irrevocable breaching of one of the last bastions of anthropocentrism' (Millet et al., 2023, p. 2). That is, the rejection of machine creativity can simply be the result of existential angst caused by AI's challenge to human exceptionality or, more precisely, Western-centric exceptionality (see, e.g., Kalpokiene & Kalpokas, 2023).

Crucially, due to the anthropocentric nature of the common takes on creativity previously outlined, generative AI, particularly when used for ostensibly creative processes, is more difficult to reconcile with existing worldviews than its uses that are more overtly mechanical, analytical, and computational in nature (Millet et al., 2023, p. 2). From a more posthumanism-informed perspective, meanwhile, creativity is best seen as distributed, removed from the domain of exclusive human agency, and instead, entangled with 'computer hardware, software, algorithms, and other tools, crafts, or knowledge on which the artist relies' (Zeilinger, 2021, p. 15). In this way, authorship is rather seen as distributed between and co-constituted by humans and artefacts (Wingström et al., 2022, p. 3). This, however, does not necessarily imply that removing the human author from the pedestal and choosing a more relational approach would somehow pave way to the recognition of AI creativity: in fact, neither would be able to occupy the coveted position of sole originator (Craig & Kerr, 2020). Hence, creative agents should be understood 'not in the traditional sense of the spirited original genius figure who produces unique creative works, but rather in a more progressive sense of creativity as a fundamentally relational, embedded, and dialogic process' (Zeilinger, 2021, p. 86). Thus understood, 'creativity becomes the ability to generate novel content by iterating derivative approximations of pre-existing materials, to the point where imitation, astonishingly, dissolves into unexpected outputs that can pass as original and, potentially, as creative' (Zeilinger, 2021, p. 86). Even without getting into the debate as to the 'proper' creativity of AI-generated content, this approach sensitises one to think beyond mere either-or dichotomic takes on creativity and delve into more complex combinations of the effects that AI might have.

By contrast, mainstream views of creativity (and resulting questions, such as what is copyrightable) are focused precisely on binary oppositions, and they often regurgitate some version of Cartesian mind-body dualism by emphasising 'intention, understanding, and rationality as prerequisites to creativity' (de Cock Buning, 2016, p. 316). Arguably, thinking about creativity appears to be 'stuck in this hardened dichotomy between real, authentic, existing creativity *versus* artificial, technological, simulated creativity' – a distinction that ultimately ends up 'revolving around a highly anthropocentric ontology based on a sharp segregation of the human and the nonhuman' (Stephensen, 2022, p. 23). Similarly, Henriksen et al. (2022, p. 466) identify creativity as being 'a fundamentally politicized concept' that 'points not only to the ideas, artifacts, processes, or products that are valued but [also] the kinds of creative emergence, ideals, or values that are deemed merit-worthy' and, by extension, discards others (primarily those seen as outside Western modernity) as unworthy.

There is a strong mainstream tendency to understand the human-machine relationship in binary terms, but as a complete opposition, (for a critique of this view, see, e.g., Broeckmann, 2019; Mellamphy, 2021; Käll, 2023), a more interactive point of view is necessary. Of course, the question of art-ness and artistic inventiveness has been extensively debated since at least the last century – a debate successively rekindled through the works of artists such as Duchamp or Warhol (Broeckmann, 2019, p. 2). Hence, although from a regulatory standpoint one might encounter the human author as the central figure, its straightforwardness is certainly debatable. After all, as Lim (2018, p. 874) alleges, both human and AI-generated works '[are] an amalgam of mimicry mined from our own learning and experience'. Similarly, for Brown (2018, p. 26), 'artists do not create in a bubble, and . . . to a certain degree, all creativity requires influence'. Still, it transpires that 'the entire legal system as it currently stands is arguably anthropocentric – indeed, strongly so', which means that 'the needs of humans . . . are always the driving force in terms of when and how to regulate activities' (Ballardini & Casi, 2020, p. 20). By extension, then, 'only human beings have intrinsic value whereas non-human natural entities possess only instrumental value and so are used as a commodity for human needs' (Ballardini & Casi, 2020, p. 20). This should come as no surprise given the strong anthropocentric bias of the Western tradition as a whole (essentially positing the human as the centre of all considerations and duties), with the corresponding legal traditions simply reflecting this normative standpoint (see, e.g., Lawrence, 2019; Käll, 2023).

It tends to be the case that although even in the domain of AI ethics and regulation 'many unquestioningly continue to emphasize human-centrism, humanism, and humanistic principles', it is significantly rarer for either researchers or practitioners to 'bother to expose the assumptions underlying human-centric narratives about human control' (Mellamphy, 2021, p. 12). Human good (or rather, a particular interpretation thereof) thus serves as the ultimate justification, despite the already evident perils of such disregard for the broader context and consequences of human actions (Lawrence, 2019, p. 24). To this effect, today's technology-focused discourse is typically characterised by an overarching drive to protect and further the gendered and racialised structures of power that have long underpinned Western societies (Jones, 2023). In fact, even the notion of 'human' or 'anthropos' should not be taken as absolute here as it contains, within its own ambit, traces of the same patterns of domination: instead one must ask, with Grear (2015, p. 227), 'who/what, precisely, *is the anthropos* of legal anthropocentrism?' A further examination reveals legal anthropocentrism to be 'a thoroughly gendered, raced construction' (Grear, 2015, p. 231) that has long excluded non-white, non-male, non-affluent, and non-neuronormative individuals (see also Kalpokiene & Kalpokas, 2023). The post-anthropocentric, post-dualist view embraced here underscores that 'historically, numerous human beings have not been fully recognized as "humans," as proved by the history of racism, sexism and colonialism, among many other frames' (Ferrando, 2020, p. 2). Only by uncovering and examining such practices, is a more productive take on creativity possible.

There are several ways in which the overall argument can proceed from here. One, which could be called 'strong' posthumanism, would interpret the enmeshment of humans and other artefacts in the achievement of goals as implying that the figure of the human author is itself out of consideration – decentred to the extent that no special treatment, including incentivisation, is necessary. After all, the human would then simply be one of a multitude of nodes, all related in an egalitarian fashion. The other approach, embraced here, could be called 'weak' posthumanism. While retaining the human author as a major figure, it sees the human author as sufficiently decentred to face significant competition. That is, the human author is insufficiently grandiose to see off any encroachment by generative AI without assistance, such as from new regulatory frameworks. Nevertheless, the human author is still considered a sufficiently important node within human societies for such help and reinforcement to be merited. Moreover, this view goes beyond allegedly value-neutral takes on technology and innovation: instead, the awareness of marginalisation and oppression with which mainstream thinking has been imbued also necessitates a closer look at the vested interests and potential wrongs of technology, thereby providing a further impetus for regulatory interventions.

Crucially, then, there is a need to go beyond simplistic assumptions whereby technology is posited to exist 'beyond the realm of values, beliefs and interests, and thus from the social world within which it resides', thereby assigning 'a blameless, agency-free inevitability to technology-driven change' that, in turn, gives rise to resignation, specifically, a sense of 'futility of resistance and the absence of alternatives' (Howcroft & Taylor, 2023, p. 353). Instead, strategies for dealing with emerging technologies need to be considered in advance, thereby ensuring that technological change and societal adaptations to it happen with those vulnerable to it (including human artists) in mind. Accordingly, the emergence of ever more sophisticated AI tools provides a new impetus 'to find new ways of encountering, discussing, and thinking of entities and environments where human and nonhuman entangle in increasingly intricate patterns' (Karkulehto et al., 2020, p. 1). Consequently, even if one admits (as one probably should) the posthumanist premise that relationality is an inescapable natural condition (Käll, 2023, p. 31), the playing field in which such relationality unfolds should not be taken for granted to be inclusive or to automatically reflect society's best interests. Instead of being beyond contestation, technological change 'includes choices, with potentially differing outcomes and implications for particular social groups with contrasting interests' (Howcroft & Taylor, 2023, p. 364). The aim of this book is to therefore take up the cause of one group involved – human authors – and to explore the ways in which their interests could be taken into account.

Bibliography

Arriagada, L. (2020). CG-Art: Demystifying the anthropocentric bias of artistic creativity. *Connection Science*, *32*(4), 398–405.

Audry, S., & Ippolito, J. (2019). Can artificial intelligence make arti without artists? Ask the viewer. *Arts*, *8*(1), 1–8.

Ballardini, R. M., & Casi, C. (2020). Regulating nature in law following weak anthropocentrism: Lessons for intellectual property regimes and environmental ethics. *Retfærd: Nordisk juridisk tidsskrift*, *167*(4), 17–38.

Benedikter, R. (2021). Can machines create art? A 'hot' topic for the future of commodified art markets. *Challenge, 64*(1), 75–86.

Bisoyi, A. (2022). Ownership, liability, patentability, and creativity in artificial intelligence. *Information and Security Journal: A Global Perspective, 31*(4), 377–386.

Boden, M. (2012). *Creativity and art: Three roads to surprise.* Oxford University Press.

Boden, M. (2016). *AI: Its nature and future.* Oxford University Press.

Bonadio, E., & McDonagh, L. (2020). *Artificial intelligence as producer and consumer of copyright works: Evaluating the consequences of algorithmic creativity.* https://papers.ssrn.com/sol3/papers.cfm?abstract_id=3617197.

Bown, O. (2021). *Beyond the creative species: Making machines that make art and music.* The MIT Press.

Boyle, J. (2003). The second enclosure movement and the construction of the public domain. *Law and Contemporary Problems, 66*, 33–74.

Broeckmann, A. (2019). The Machine Artist as Myth. *Arts, 8*, 1–10.

Brown, N. I. (2018). Artificial Authors: A Case for Copyright in Computer-Generated Works. *Columbia Science and Technology Law Review, 20*(1), 1–41.

Craig, C., & Kerr, I. (2020). The death of the AI author. *Ottawa Law Review, 52*(1), 31–86.

de Cock Buning, M. (2016). Autonomous Intelligent Systems as Creative Agents under the EU Framework for Intellectual Property. *European Journal of Risk Regulation, 7*(2), 310–322.

De Cremer, D., Bianzino, N. M., & Falk, B. (2023, April 13). How generative AI could disrupt creative work. *Harvard Business Review.* https://hbr.org/2023/04/how-generative-ai-could-disrupt-creative-work.

DiBlasi, J. (2022). Tuning topological morphologies: Creative processes of natural and artificial cognitive systems. In C. Vear & F. Poltronieri (Eds.), *The language of creative AI: Practices, aesthetics and structures* (pp. 235–257). Springer.

Drott, E. (2021). Copyright, compensation, and commons in the music AI industry. *Creative Industries Journal, 14*(2), 190–207.

Du Sautoy, M. (2020). *The creativity code: How AI is learning to write, paint and think.* 4th Estate.

Eisikovits, N., & Stubbs, A. (2023, January 12). ChatGPT, DALL-E and the collapse of the creative process. *The Conversation.* https://theconversation.com/chatgpt-dall-e-2-and-the-collapse-of-the-creative-process-196461.

Ferrando, F. (2020). Leveling the posthuman playing field. *Theology and Science, 18*(1), 1–6.

Geiger, C., & Iaia, V. (2024). The forgotten creator: Towards a statutory remuneration right for machine learning of generative AI. *Computer Law & Security Review: The International Journal of Technology Law and Practice, 52*, 1–9.

Grear, A. (2015). Deconstructing anthropos: A critical legal reflection on 'anthropocentric' law and anthropocene 'humanity'. *Law Critique, 26*, 225–249.

Guadamuz, A. (2021). Do androids dream of electric copyright? Comparative analysis of originality in artificial intelligence generated works. In I. J.-A. Lee, R. Hilty, & K.-C. Liu (Eds.), *Artificial intelligence and intellectual property* (pp. 147–176). Oxford University Press.

Henriksen, D., Creely, E., & Mehta, R. (2022). Rethinking the politics of creativity: Posthumanism, indigeneity, and creativity beyond the Western anthropocene. *Qualitative Inquiry, 28*(5), 465–475.

Hertzmann, A. (2018). Can computers create art? *Arts, 7*, 1–25.

Howcroft, D., & Taylor, P. (2023). Automation and the future of work: A social shaping of technology approach. *New Technology, Work and Employment, 38*, 351–370.

Jones, E. (2023). Posthuman Feminism and Global Constitutionalism: Environmental Reflections. *Global Constitutionalism, 12*(3), 495–509.

Käll, J. (2023). *Posthuman property and law: Commodification and control through information, smart spaces and artificial intelligence.* Routledge.

Kalpokiene, J., & Kalpokas, I. (2023). Creative encounters of a posthuman kind: Anthropocentric law, artificial intelligence, and art. *Technology in Society, 72*. https://doi.org/10.1016/j.techsoc.2023.10219.

Karkulehto, S., Koistinen, A.-K., Lummaa, K., & Varis, E. (2020). Reconfiguring human, nonhuman and posthuman: Striving for more ethical cohabitation. In S. Karkulehto, A.-K. Koistinen, & E. Varis (Eds.), *Reconfiguring Human, Nonhuman and Posthuman in Literature and Culture* (pp. 1–19). Routledge.

Lawrence, M. (2019). Anthropocentrism does not fit: Proofs from history, science, and logic for ecocentric attorneys. *Journal of Animal & Environmental Law, 11*(1), 16–27.

Lee, H-K. (2022). Rethinking creativity: Creative industries, AI and everyday creativity. *Media, Culture & Society, 44*(3), 601–612.

Lim, D. (2018). AI & IP: Innovation creativity in an age of accelerated change. *Akron Law Review, 52*(3), 813–876.

Mellamphy, N. B. (2021). Humans "in the loop"? Human-centrism, posthumanism, and AI. *Nature and Culture, 16*(1), 11–27.

Millet, K., Buehler, F., Du, G., & Kokkoris, M. D. (2023). Defending humankind: Anthropocentric bias in the appreciation of AI art. *Computers in Human Behavior, 143*, 1–9.

Morreale, F. (2021). Where does the buck stop? Ethical and political issues with AI in music creation. *Transactions of the International Society for Music Information Retrieval, 4*(1), 105–113.

Moruzzi, C. (2020). Artificial Creativity and General Intelligence. *Journal of Science and Technology of the Arts, 12*(3), 84–99.

Munden, D. (2022, November 7). Generative AI: Copyright and Computer-Generated Images. *Columbia University Science and Technology Law Review,* https://journals.library.columbia.edu/index.php/stlr/blog/view/462.

Murray, M. D. (2023). Generative and AI authored artworks and copyright law. *Hastings Communications and Entertainment Law Journal, 45*(1), 27–44.

Naqvi, Z. (2020). Artificial intelligence, copyright, and copyright infringement. *Marquette Intellectual Property Law Review, 24*(1), 15–52.

Natale, S. (2022). The lovelace effect: Perceptions of creativity in machines. *New Media & Society*. https://doi.org/10.1177/14614448221077278.

Newton, A., & Dhole, K. (2023). Is AI art another industrial revolution in the making? *arXiv*. https://arxiv.org/abs/2301.05133.

Paquette, L. (2021). Artificial life imitating art imitating life: Copyright ownership in AI-generated works. *Intellectual Property Journal, 33*, 183–215.

Picht, P. G., & Thouvenin, F. (2023). AI and IP: Theory to policy and back again – Policy and research recommendations at the intersection of artificial intelligence and intellectual property. *IIC – International Review of Intellectual Property and Competition Law, 54*, 916–940.

Poltronieri, F. (2022). Towards a symbiotic future: Art and creative AI. In C. Vear & F. Poltronieri (Eds.), *The language of creative AI: Practices, aesthetics and structures* (pp. 29–40). Springer.

Potts, J. (2023). *The near-death of the author: Creativity in the internet age*. The University of Toronto Press.

Ramalho, A. (2022). *Intellectual property protection for AI-generated creations: Europe, the United States, Australia and Japan*. Routledge.

Sætra, H. S. (2023). Generative AI: Here to stay, but for good? *Technology in Society, 75*, 1–5.

Senftleben, M. (2023). Generative AI and author remuneration. *IIC – International Review of Intellectual Property and Competition Law, 54*, 1535–1560.

Shtefan, A. (2021). Creativity and artificial intelligence: A view from the perspective of copyright. *Journal of Intellectual Property Law & Practice, 16*(7), 720–728.

Spindler, G. (2022). AI and copyright law: The European perspective. In L. A. Di Matteo, C. Poncibò, & M. Cannarsa (Eds.), *The Cambridge handbook of artificial intelligence: Global perspectives on law and ethics* (pp. 257–269). Cambridge University Press.

Stephensen, J. L. (2022). Artificial creativity: Beyond the human, or beyond definition? *Transformations, 36*, 19–37.

Tredinnick, L., & Laybats, C. (2023). The dangers of generative artificial intelligence. *Business Information Review, 40*(2), 46–48.

Tubadji, A., Huang, H., & Webber, D. J. (2021). Cultural proximity bias in AI-acceptability: The Importance of being human. *Technological Forecasting & Social Change, 173*, 1–14.

Wingström, R., Hautala, J., & Lundman, R. (2022). Redefining creativity in the Era of AI? Perspectives of computer scientists and new media artists. *Creativity Research Journal*. https://doi.org/10.1080/10400419.2022.2107850.

Zeilinger, M. (2021). *Tactical entanglements: AI art, creative agency, and the limits of intellectual property*. Meson Press.

2 AI and the Creative Industries

Challenges and Opportunities

In some ways and contexts, it is already increasingly the case that 'humans share the canvas with another talented artist – Artificial Intelligence' (Škiljić, 2021, p. 1339). Certainly, not all subscribe to the view of AI-generated output being revolutionary in the arts and creative industries. Broeckmann (2019, p. 3), for example, instead takes a more evolutionary approach by claiming that generative AI tools 'may contribute to the continuous transformation of sense-making that we tend to categorise as "art"'. This might nevertheless still be sufficient to transform human incentives for artistic creativity. However, notably, the impact of generative AI on the livelihoods and incentive structures of authors is likely to be uneven. Although the impact of AI might be felt less by already famous and influential artists, it is the up-and-coming creators and those labouring in the creative industries who would be affected the most (Volpicelli, 2023). Hence, the focus of this chapter is on AI's potential to displace particularly human artists and those labouring in the creative industries. Of course, it is acknowledged that AI may also open new and heretofore not present opportunities and streams of revenue, thus enabling those having different skills to reap financial gains.

2.1 AI, Creativity, and the Author: Some Complications

Clearly, digital technologies have already significantly transformed the ways in which creative industries operate. On the user side, they have considerably reduced the cost of discovery and access, first through downloading and subsequently through streaming; on the creation side, both creation and distribution costs and times have been reduced while access to audience data has provided the opportunity to more effectively tailor content to user preferences (Peukert, 2019, p. 199). After all, machine learning capacities mean that such models are fundamentally socially intertwined instead of existing in some separate virtual realm (Arriagada, 2020). Generative AI adds a further intensification of tailoring, with technology companies acquiring the ability not only to select from existing content but also to generate content on demand. Consequently, instead of being

DOI: 10.4324/9781003464976-2

restricted to the consumption of existing works, audiences may find themselves with the luxury of having endless variations of what they already like being generated in real time for their own personalised consumption to an extent that no human artist (or even a team thereof) would be able to achieve (Bown, 2021, pp. 6–7; De Cremer et al., 2023). Given the importance of satisfying audience preferences and the need to do so quickly (due to near-instant content distribution channels and, consequently, ever shorter audience attention spans), resorting to AI generation appears to be an attractive option, since AI tools can automatically gauge preferences, tailor their output accordingly, and put the end result up for distribution – all at machine speed (Peukert, 2019, p. 202). Creative content producers would then end up in a race to undercut one another in satisfying the next upcoming craving just a little bit quicker – a cultural industry version of flash trading on financial markets. From a strictly technology-focused perspective, this might seem as a natural and even desirable development. For example, as Lim (2018, p. 854) rhetorically asks, '[i]f AI can learn from the greatest books, movies, and music we have to offer and create work that supersedes what has come before, how is that not both technological and aesthetic progress?' Nevertheless, such developments would largely remove the human author and human creativity from the supply of content to audiences.

Drott (2021, pp. 201–202) makes an important point: the focus on harms has been understood on an individual level (one forger or copyright infringer harming one artist), but the power of AI lies in its capacity for generalisation and abstraction, which means that 'the potential market harms of commercial AI are not located at an individual level, but at a population level', which undermines the position of human authors *as such* rather than individual creators or their works. Therefore, despite creative acts having been traditionally associated with human beings, the emergence of generative AI has challenged such long-held assumptions as machines have become able to 'create books, music, paintings and other subject matter that would come under copyright protection when created by a human being', thereby raising important questions regarding both the status and the impact of such outputs (Ramalho, 2022, p. 6). Indeed, it is important to emphasise, as Zatarain (2017, p. 91) does, that although '[t]raditionally, technical extensions were used as a mere extension of human creativity and invention' completely guided by and helping further extend human intentionality, such a simplistic perspective may well be upended by the development of ever more advanced AI tools. After all, as argued by Mazzone and Elgammal (2019, p. 5), the Holy Grail of those working on (ostensibly) creative AI is 'developing *machine* process and *machine* creativity, not merely aping and trying to pass as human-made'. Should these be achieved, an important milestone towards the acceptance of AI creativity would also be achieved (another achievement would be AI's independent will or desire to create).

Already, the development of generative AI capacities can be seen as a major threat to both the idea of an author's unique personality (as something akin to that which can be reproduced from data) and material incentives (as AI-generated output can limit the ways for human authors to monetise their works), thereby significantly affecting the landscape of human creativity (Degli Eposti et al., 2020). Admittedly, there are still doubts as to how truly independent AI-enabled tools may reasonably become and, therefore, as to whether substitution or *augmentation* of human creativity might be the actual outcome (see, e.g., Anantrasirichai & Bull, 2022). Some authors, meanwhile, are already inclined to claim that AI-generated outputs would soon become superior to human-created ones due to AI's capacity to learn from vast amounts of human creations (see, e.g., Davenport & Mittal, 2022), with generative AI's output ultimately extending beyond existing styles and conventions (Millet et al., 2023, p. 1). AI is alleged to be able to offer a completely different and unexpected (non-human) take on the vast numbers of human-created artworks; moreover, being able to also learn what humans tend to like, AI can tailor the results to prevalent tastes, which has led some authors to claim that AI 'can make new things that are relatable and comprehensible but, at the same time, completely unexpected' (Kelly, 2022). This technological optimism is, of course, not uncontested, not even taking into account its one-sidedness (conspicuously leaving the impact on human authors out of consideration). Furthermore, due to their capacity to learn from and produce diverse content, generative AI tools have the potential to become 'universal content machines' and thus replacing entire creative teams (Davenport & Mittal, 2022; De Cremer et al., 2023; see also Walzer, 2023). Indeed, the malleability of generative AI systems and the possibility of stretching their use across multiple and diverse contexts enable a scale of application that exceeds other types of currently available AI (Helberger & Diakopoulos, 2023, p. 2).

At the very least, AI can significantly compress the creative process not only by eliminating the need for human learning and skill development but also by reducing the actual time of output production into machinic speeds (Sun et al., 2023; see also De Cremer et al., 2023). Even the apparent flaws of existing technology, such as common rendering errors, have the potential to be absorbed into contemporary digital culture, ultimately becoming new aesthetic conventions (O'Meara & Murphy, 2023). All of this points towards a future where 'a significant portion of hitherto human creative output will be produced by AI', with artificial creativity ending up determining 'an ever larger area of art, culture, and public communication and information' (Dornis, 2020, p. 42). As Lim (2018, p. 854) bluntly puts it, '[s]ome outclassed human creators will find their livelihoods challenged if they are unwilling to retrain, retool, and use AI to augment their work to remain relevant' – which is in no way different from the challenges that workers in most other industries are facing.

The substitution argument nevertheless significantly depends on the appreciation of AI-generated content and the value ascribed to it (or lack thereof). As noted earlier, the function (and according to some, use-value) of AI-generated content could be identical (or even superior) to that of human-created works, but the more theoretical discussion typically tends to be less favourable to AI. When discussing creativity and particularly the capability of AI to be creative, there is a tendency to resort to rather grand claims about the exceptionality of creative acts, that is, 'the ruptures and discontinuities that mark the work of great artists' and the ways in which '[c]reativity erupts where the unpredictable enters into the work of art' (Nowotny, 2022, p. 48). Likewise, following Boden's (2012, p. 29) influential account, '[c]reativity is the ability to come up with ideas or artefacts that are *new, surprising, and valuable*'. In this sense, although generative AI could efficiently produce output that is continuous of past creative efforts as manifested in the training data, 'real' creativity lies in *dis*continuity. Notably, current AI models have been developed to emulate the way that human information processing works. For example, '[w]hile people may identify and untangle different semantic aspects of what they see subconsciously, neural networks can exhibit similar behaviour after learning from a large enough collection of samples' by identifying the features salient in a specific dataset; still, such similarities are rarely seen as sufficient to equate human and machine creativity (Bolojan, 2022, p. 25).

Among the theoretical attempts to make sense of and classify creativity, particularly regarding AI, Boden's tripartite definition (see, e.g., Boden, 2016, pp. 68–69) has probably attracted the most attention. In order of increasing value, it includes the following: first, combinatorial creativity, which involves merely regurgitating already familiar ideas and rearranging (or recombining) them in a new (but largely unsurprising) way; second, exploratory creativity, which operates within existing conventions but nevertheless pushes the boundaries by coming up with novel ideas; and finally, transformational creativity, which breaks the existing rules and styles to create something that is new in both form and content. The implication for generative AI, then, is that it can be safely assumed to master the first and sometimes even the second type of creativity, while the final one remains out of reach. This conceptualisation can be seen as raising the bar very high, even to the extent of hardly reflecting what happens in the context of the economisation of creativity, which is characteristic of the creative industries as described in the following discussion. Illustratively, Boden (2012, p. 181) also identifies three kinds of autonomy of artistic agents: the first describes the response to an agent's environment on the continuum between directness (reacting to the world as it manifests itself at the moment) and indirectness (mediated by previous history); the second type refers to the ability to self-direct, that is, to set one's own priorities rather than have them imposed from the outside; finally, the third is the capacity to independently tailor one's practices regarding the specific problem at hand. In this context, algorithmic creativity is seen as bounded and more akin to imitation (Amoore, 2020, pp. 89–90). The content produced by generative AI is certainly not accidental (as it is the result of machine learning processes and not a mere random distribution of pixels, words, or sounds), but it is also not intentional: quite usefully, Brainard (2023) gives the example of a houseplant that grows towards the light neither by accident nor by some conscious intention. Instead, both the plant and a generative AI model are determined by their intrinsic qualities that are natural and artificial, respectively. However, the complexity of generative models and the large number of parameters involved means that such a determination is complex: instead of following pre-existing rules and procedures, they build on and form patterns and connections identified at the training stage, thereby producing results that are quasi-spontaneous (Brainard, 2023).

Generative AI is based on the analysis of existing data and patterns that are then replicated and rearranged on a statistical basis; humans are allegedly capable of creating new works without a template or reference to what already exists, whereas AI-generated output must always be based on something prior and is never *ex nihilo* (Shtefan, 2021, p. 727). Creativity is thus seen as 'the exclusive prerogative of humans' – something that remains out of reach for AI tools, even if the output of AI could, under some conditions or criteria, 'have great value to society' (Shtefan, 2021, p. 728). The value of a 'true' artwork is also seen to be not merely in the work itself but in the skill and the struggle in finding the right expression for the underlying idea, while generative AI tools are then criticised for simply making the process too easy and painless, thus allegedly leading to a 'collapse' of creativity (Eisikovits & Stubbs, 2023). The absence of both intrinsic motivation and the capacity of feeling emotion would then deprive the output of its 'humanity' (Sun et al., 2023). According to this line of argumentation, '[w]hen constructing an object, AI does not express anything, does not put a message in this object and does not seek to convey something to the world, because it does not have such ability' (Shtefan, 2021, p. 728). This, however, is an overly stark observation that does not take into account the interactivity of a work, namely, the way that it is constituted *as a work* and acquires meaning (what it is intended to convey) in the interplay among the object itself, the appreciating subject, and the circumstances of such interaction (see, e.g., Kalpokas, 2023).

It could also be argued that current views on creativity are neither neutral nor atemporal. Instead, the way that art and creativity are conceptualised dates back to Romanticism and its tendency to focus on exceptionality and genius, thereby according artists 'a special place in society' due to their alleged capacity to express hidden inner layers of their own personality and the universalities of humanity, which posits art itself as uniquely human (Manovich, 2022: 62; see also Mazzone & Elgammal, 2019; Moruzzi, 2021). Because of the dominant Romantic view of art and creativity, creativity is something that 'comes from the inside, from [artists'] imagination' and can thus be seen as free-flowing from persons endowed with this special capacity (Manovic, 2022, p. 62). The currently dominant view embraces the idea of 'heroic creativity' as a sequence of great masters and disruptors, be it Bach or the Beatles (Stephenson, 2022, p. 23; see also Potts, 2023, pp. 15–16). Indeed, the mainstream notion of creativity is particularly evident when compared to another mode of production – that of making things. In this dualism, making things is understood as something simple and mundane and as production of the same or similar thing multiple times without significant qualitative differentiation, whereas creativity is typically associated with bringing about something fundamentally new whereby every output is qualitatively different from others, not only vis-à-vis the author's own output but also from an art-historical point of view (Bown, 2021, p. 44). However, the historically specific notion of this heroic view also implies that the currently taken-for-granted arts and creativity nexus and the privilege generally awarded to human creativity and authorship (both its practices and outcomes) are only 'relatively recent inventions' (Manovich, 2022, p. 65).

Just like all heroic stories, such an account of irruptions of creativity is in itself a myth, with authors more likely flourishing through a continuous process of interaction and growth instead of meteoric emergence (Du Sautoy, 2020, p. 15). The search for inner qualities that underpin creativity, whether it is 'talent' or 'inspiration', is not without its critics either: Arriagada (2020, p. 400) notably refers to these as 'mystical qualities' that give rise to a 'mystical version of art'. In a similar fashion, Moruzzi (2021, p. 2) criticises the idea of a 'creative person' as 'an extraordinary individual . . . who possesses the mysterious gift of creating something that ordinary people are not capable of'. By following such critical perspectives, creativity would be more akin to the connection and recombination of already existing building blocks (Potts, 2023, p. 154). An alternative notion of creativity, then, might be one that focuses on creativity as a social process and interaction; this shifts the question from 'how a given entity *is creative*' to the less ontologically loaded question of 'what role an entity plays in [its] contribution to a larger creative process' (Bown, 2021, p. 75). Such a reformulation is significantly more inclusive of AI models that, despite lacking conscious and intentional origination, can nevertheless and do contribute to the broader landscape of creativity. This, in turn, is not merely an issue of abstract debate but also one of the reasons why generative AI is likely to have a major impact on individual authors and on the creative industries as an organised process of creative content production regardless of the characteristics of this technology at any given time.

Likewise, concerning the intentionality of creativity, a question could be asked as to the extent to which such self-determination of priorities and practices is possible even for human artists given the market pressures and the necessity for many artists to work within the constraints of the creative industries. Moreover, it must be admitted that human creativity is not unlimited but is instead restricted by previous experience: just like AI models can extrapolate from training data, humans can extrapolate from their experience. That is, '[t]he boundaries of your imagination are sculpted from your perceptions of the world' (Crespo & McCormick, 2022, p. 56). It transpires that there is a tendency to romanticise and aggrandise creativity, often at the expense of considering the co-constitution of creativity in which humans, artefacts, technologies, cultural and societal contexts, and other factors participate; this more interactive, co-constitutive, approach allows for the participation of *both* humans and AI in the creative process without diminishing the outcome (Wingström et al., 2022). Instead, generative AI may end up revealing that '[c] reativity is not some supernatural force' but instead, 'something that can be synthesized, amplified, and manipulated' (Kelly, 2022), thereby underscoring the complexity in isolating the human and the technological domains.

Regardless of the outcome of this debate, it is clear that human authors face greater competition from AI than from their fellow humans because the 'AI-generation of new creations based on a training set can be unleashed with low marginal costs, and can explore any kind of combinations and variations' (Degli Eposti et al., 2020, p. 67). Hence, even if potential buyers are willing to pay less for AI-generated output (as discussed later in this book), the commercial viability of AI generation would likely still hold. Crucially, even in the case of AI-generated output being of lower quality (irrespective of the actual definition of lower quality), human creators can still be crowded out – 'drowned out by a tsunami of algorithmically generated content' – and unable to compete against cheap and plentiful alternatives (De Cremer et al., 2023). Moreover, one can expect a turning point when the sheer amount of AI-generated content would start causing a shift in what is taken as normal and acceptable – and perhaps the understanding of quality itself – potentially bringing the 'aggregate and statistical reasoning' of generative AI tools to the status of a standard for creative practice (Atkinson & Barker, 2023). After all, it must be reiterated that the competition over audience attention is already very intense, 'and this kind of competition – and pressure – will only rise further if there is unlimited content on demand' (De Cremer et al., 2023). Therefore, whoever (or *what*ever) can prevail in the competitive struggle will end up defining the new era of creativity.

2.2   Creative Industries and the Propensity for Human Substitution

The move from creativity towards creative industries is enabled by the specifically Western understanding of creativity: one that is individualised, legitimises human dominance over the rest of the world (rendering the world as mere material for human creativity to take shape), and is focused on marketisation and economic value extraction (see, notably, Henriksen et al., 2022, p. 473). The rise in prominence of the creative industries, both as part of political discourse and as an economic sector, has since its inception been premised on the allegedly unlimited resource of creative inventiveness, with the ensuing expectation of equally unlimited economic outcomes; nevertheless, such thinking has always been based on an occlusion of the precarity and low income that characterised the life conditions of the employees in such industries (Lee, 2022, p. 603). A common assumption when considering creative industries 'assumes unrestricted economic growth that is driven by the abundance of productive human creativity'; nevertheless, the reality is that human creativity can be scarce, and the process of bringing it to a tangible expression (i.e., the production of a copyrightable work) can be inefficient, leading creative industry companies into cut-throat global competition in the contemporary media and cultural condition that is characterised by a scarcity of attention (Lee, 2022, p. 604). As Lee (2022, p. 604) emphasises, '[a]rtistic and cultural production – singing, acting, drawing, writing, etc. – tends to be labour-intensive'. That is, of course, unless it is automated so that efficiency is maximised (Nowotny, 2022, p. 22). Hence, from an industry-commercial point of view, the use of AI tools presents a solution by replacing labour with capital in the production of cultural output (Lee, 2022, p. 605). In fact, generative AI's success, when applied in the creative industries, is 'not likely to be about the *persuasiveness* and *human-likeness* of the generated music' but instead, about 'efficiency in driving down the cost of creative labour' (Morreale, 2021, p. 108). After all, notably, '[m]ost human art, past and present, has been lowercase' which is 'exactly what the AI generators deliver' (Kelly, 2022). There is already evidence of AI's capacity to replace entire departments in creative industry companies and significantly cut down the time necessary for achieving the desired result (Heaven, 2022).

Evidently, the industry standard for the protection of human creators was already low even prior to the emergence of generative AI. There is then a clear contradiction at the heart of creative industries: 'on the one side, optimistic promises of creative labour as liberating, self-expressive and autonomous, and on the other the rampant precarity and inequality which plagues the sector' (Marčeta et al., 2023, p. 2). Thus, overall, a paradox in the creative industries moving to the mainstream cannot be lost: 'what was earlier considered an exception or even alternative to the capitalist mode of production due to the prevalence of both non-standard work and passionate workers pursing self-expression, has become a role-model' (Marčeta et al., 2023, p. 2) but with detrimental effects to the creators involved.

Creativity has thus become a form of capital 'that can be accumulated, is put into the production process and is easily transferrable across different sectors' (Lee, 2022, p. 603). This economisation of creativity may have laid the foundation for creativity's subsequent substitution with automated content generation. Meanwhile, for the companies involved in the creative industries, 'copyright in popular works serves as if it is capital by generating income for many years and being invested in producing attractive new cultural commodities', therefore creating a vicious circle towards ever more centralised power (Lee, 2022, p. 603). Generally, then, individuals and businesses involved in the creative industries can be seen to produce 'goods and services with a culturally significant artistic content', leading to the two-pronged nature of this domain: 'production on an industrial scale and cultural content' (Cacciatore

& Panozzo, 2022, p. 2). 2022: 1; see also Papadimitriou et al., 2022, p. 4; Khlystova & Kalyuzhnova, 2023). The focus of creative industries increasingly seems to be on the industry rather than on the creative aspect of the term, emphasising their role in job creation and economic growth, whereby human creative capacities and the intellectual property resulting from them become objects of economic exploitation via new managerial techniques (Gonzalez-Cristiano & Le Grand, 2023, p. 1; see also Alacovska, 2022, p. 676; Haugsevje, 2022). The introduction of generative AI (presumably in the hands of the existing corporate players or fast-growing newcomers, i.e., startups) only further strengthens this propensity towards concentration. After all, for the corporate actors involved in the creative industries, generative AI can resolve the occlusion noted previously but at the expense of human authors: despite the seeming abundance and unlimited nature of creativity, there are still barriers to growth that originate from the laboriousness of human creativity, whereas the generative potential of AI is effectively unlimited. Moreover, this entire transition may happen unnoticed by the consumers of these creative outputs; for example, an increasing amount of AI-generated content (music both composed and performed by AI) can creep into playlists on Spotify without there being any notable objection from the users.

Central to the creative industries is the interrelationship between economic value, on the one hand, and cultural, economic, and artistic values, on the other hand (Gohoungodji & Amara, 2023), thereby tying creativity to economic performance (Papadimitriou et al., 2022, p. 4). Consequently, any notion of art for art's sake is replaced by an interplay among creativity, feasibility (in terms such as institutional and material resources), and societal/market conditions in determining what exactly ends up being created (Paris & Mahmoud-Jouini, 2019, p. 405). Accordingly, the effects of generative AI are likely to be significant. If the economic exploitation of creative capacities and the results of creative labour are at the crux of the creative industries, then the individuals working there (and knowledge and creative workers more broadly) face the same or very similar threats of substitution with AI as industrial workers in other domains. Moreover, substitution is only part of the problem because even if it does not fully take place, 'there is a risk that work changes, and whenever this occurs we need to be wary of how power constellations change and whether such changes are conducive to the decency of work' (Sætra, 2023, p. 3). Accordingly, even in the absence of full substitution, marginalisation and further alienation of creative workers from the content they create (or help AI to create) would be a likely outcome.

By contrast, Zhao and Zhang (2023), for example, postulate an optimistic take on the relationship between AI and the creative industries by focusing on tackling traditionally slow artistic productivity, expanding the workforce through the democratisation of creativity, and thus incentivising growth (a similar perspective is also found in Khlystova & Kalyuzhnova, 2023). After all, the creative industries have always been focused (and perhaps even premised) on the adoption of new, particularly digital, technologies, including in terms of content creation and delivery to the end user (Khlystova & Kalyuzhnova, 2023; Szakálné Kanó et al., 2023). Likewise, such developments could to some extent be normalised by emphasising that intensive competition and operation in a constantly shifting market constitute a need for permanent innovation and change in the creative industries (Wohl, 2021). Especially, the push to permanently produce new products and content (Gohoungodji & Amara, 2023) makes the creative industries particularly susceptible to AI-enabled efficiencies.

The emphasis on the creative industries as fundamentally innovation-focused also extends to seeing them as driving not only economic but also societal growth (Cacciatore & Panozzo, 2022; see also Wohl, 2021). Of course, should such innovation be outsourced to AI to a significant degree, questions could be raised as to which values and considerations are actually behind the ongoing societal developments and whether or not humans are losing control of their own societies, at least from a cultural perspective. Likewise, such technology focus undergirds a tension between local embeddedness and globalisation, meaning that the creative industries cannot be completely sheltered from global processes and trends even in cases when their operational focus is local or regional (Szakálné Kanó et al., 2023).

Creative industries are prone to risk and operate in an uncertain market because they are dependent on ever-shifting audience beliefs and preferences – their product offerings are typically based on experiential and symbolic value propositions rather than on objective and tangible use-value (Paris & Mahmoud-Jouini, 2019, p. 404). Indeed, organisations in the creative industries are subjected to, as Sigurdardottir and Candi (2019, p. 477) aptly call it, 'an accordion growth strategy', which means that 'firms are allowed to grow and shrink as needed – whether in response to external conditions or the (dis)appearance of opportunities for artistic production'. Of course, this flexibility comes at the expense of work stability for people engaged in this domain. Hence, engagement in the creative industries tends to involve significant precarity whereby all the risk and effects of market fluctuations are passed on directly to the human creators despite them having very limited recourse to social protection (O'Brien & Arnold, 2022, p. 2). Artists are already facing a situation whereby the majority of them are only receiving a meagre share of income from online platforms and other intermediaries; thus, they struggle to live off their work (Lee, 2022, p. 603; see also Been et al., 2023). Particularly in the context of the platformisation of content supply, high levels of popularity (e.g., in the form of streams) are necessary for remuneration to kick in, and even then at a very low rate (Patrickson, 2021, p. 588). Moreover, in terms of economic rewards, particularly groups that are already underprivileged tend to be the worst affected by the lack of stability and security in the creative industries (Been et al., 2023). The creative industries have also been among the pioneers driving the growth of freelance work (Gonzalez-Cristiano & Le Grand, 2023, p. 1).

There are also more optimistic accounts, whereby the previously described precarity has been reframed as a shift towards an entrepreneurial version of creativity populated by 'individuals whose primary life goal is to build an artistic career by creating new products and services' while producing 'economic capital to sustain their career aspirations' (Papadimitriou et al., 2022, p. 3). This also leads to a drive towards greater 'professionalisation' in the creative industries, which is usually synonymous with greater market orientation (Haugsevje, 2022, p. 13). Nevertheless, AI's capacity to dissociate creativity from human effort and labour tends to undermine any ideas of human authors as content entrepreneurs since the human factor can be eliminated altogether (Lee, 2022, p. 605). Meanwhile, application of generative AI in the creative industries offers lucrative opportunities for corporate actors given not only the low cost of content generation but also AI's lack of awareness and independence: although humans can organise themselves and demand better treatment, AI's lack of consciousness and personality precludes such capacity (Morreale, 2021, p. 108). Hence, the business benefits of driving down costs and significantly increasing volume are obvious (Newton & Dhole, 2023).

As Zeilinger (2021, p. 13) emphasises, AI 'tends to serve socio-economic regimes that rely on the automation, high-speed calculation, data-intensive analysis, predictive techniques, and communicative abilities that computation affords'. The current status of creative work, particularly as it pertains to the creative industries, certainly fits the brief. Such conditions set the scene for what could be seen as unavoidable human-AI competition, in which human artists have little chance of prevailing (Morreale, 2021). Crucially, AI might render skill and practice superfluous, not only dispersing but also trivialising creativity (Eisikovits & Stubbs, 2023). Others, meanwhile, would assert a contrary position by, emphasising how generative AI could offer novel ideals, alternative ways of thinking, and new ways of engaging with audiences, thereby significantly benefitting the creative industries and even the individuals employed therein (Tennakoon, 2022). Nevertheless, the line between augmentation and substitution remains very thin even in such accounts.

AI's ability to mimic specific styles (not just general trends but also specific artists) means that even prolific established authors are not safe from (significantly cheaper) substitution with AI – particularly since in jurisdictions such as the US, only specific works but not the style of an artist are protectable (Nolan, 2022). Nevertheless, the matter of ascribed value once again enters the fore, with audience capacity and willingness to project value onto AI-generated content returning to the spotlight (see, e.g., Natale, 2022, p. 2). Notably, appreciation of art (human created or AI-generated) is a highly subjective issue and is highly dependent on personal preferences and tastes, the prior experience and knowledge of each individual in question, and contextual factors – not only the history and reputation of the work and the artist (if any) but also, pertaining to AI-generated content, the appreciating individual's opinion about AI and its creative potential (Messingschlager & Appel, 2023, p. 2). Perception of meaning is also key, although other aspects tend to be more controversial: for example, Messingschlager and Appel (2023, p. 2) also add the requirement of art being perceived as beautiful and aesthetically pleasing, but this would arguably disqualify much of modern art, which can often be intentionally provocative or disconcerting. Notably, moreover, the quality or merit of the work is irrelevant for its copyrightability. Hence, creativity is not 'in the internal functioning of the machine' but instead, 'an attribution of human users that might be stimulated also through non-technical elements such as context, cultural expectations and social dynamics' (Natale, 2022, p. 2). Even when focusing narrowly on the creative industries, there is proof of the importance of a match and rapport between artists and buyers or clients (see, e.g., Gonzalez-Cristiano & Le Grand, 2023), and clearly such rapport can hardly be built with (at least the current version of) AI. Nevertheless, given the very low cost of AI-enabled content generation, a rebalancing of such otherwise human-focused priorities does appear to be a realistic possibility. Therefore, simple cost-benefit calculations are likely to play an important role.

Crucially, automation-induced cost savings in the creative industries are likely to be such that it would still pay off to use AI even in cases when it performs worse than humans (Svedman, 2020, p. 14; see also Dignam, 2020, p. 44; Naqvi, 2020). In the context of artistic production, even if AI-produced works are seen as less valuable (aesthetically and/or monetarily) and not subject to copyright, it would still make sense, particularly for large corporate investors, to flood the market with AI-generated outputs (art and other creative content). Churning out even cheaper and less-valued items in bulk would be sufficient for technology companies but still disastrous to human authors. Furthermore, creative industries are already significantly premised upon 'a tension between creative work and business' (Gonzalez-Cristiano & Le Grand, 2023, p. 12), which signifies a tendency to economise human creativity while generative AI offers economies of scale in the creative process (Tigre Moura et al., 2023). This is all perfectly aligned with the 'industry' aspect of the creative industries.

Regardless of what one thinks of the quality of AI-generated content, its definite advantages are quantity and price: as cheap artworks enter the market, human artists would find themselves hardly able to compete, while companies (and, presumably, other artists) using AI would still be able to profit due to high levels of AI productivity (Kinsella, 2021; see also Kulp, 2020; Naqvi, 2020). In this sense, the critique of AI art as merely playing with form (see Elgammal, 2020) may simply be going too high and too elitist: for the average consumer, it is likely that price and convenience would be more important in making purchase decisions in a manner not dissimilar from the relationship between mass-produced and artisanal goods in other market segments. This is rather clearly demonstrated by the drive of platforms such as Spotify to search for ways of using AI to generate their own content, based on the troves of content and the user taste data available to them (see, e.g., Fergus, 2020). In fact, content could well end up being generated in real time for each user's personal consumption in accordance with their taste data (Bown, 2021, p. 6), thereby removing or reducing the need for human artists in the traditional practice of creating content for a broader audience in advance.

As Velthuis (2013, p. 37) asserts, the value of art is socially constructed in the first place as 'it is a market based on the production of belief' heavily affected by institutions such as galleries, museums, the media, etc. that frame and contextualise particular works and assert their value (or refuse to do so); by making 'a selection out of the large "pool" of oeuvres and individual artworks', they ascribe symbolic and, therefore, monetary value. Seen in this light, the future of art markets and the creative industries – and the place of humans in them – rests not on some predetermined characteristics of the work or its author but on the way in which such institutional gatekeepers frame AI and human works. However, one could also reasonably claim that such gatekeeping functions are also being transformed because digital technologies (particularly online platforms) have made the searching (often replaced by simple acceptance of algorithmically generated recommendations) and acquisition of works not only much easier but also dependent on the algorithmic logics of discovery (Peukert 2019, pp. 199–200). Crucially, such automated forms of curation also tend to be agnostic as to the origin of the content promoted or demoted in the algorithmic pecking order.

Given their capacity to know what would sell in advance of the content even having been created and their capacity to invest in and develop generative AI agents, large technology and platform companies seem to be bound to become both creators and gatekeepers simultaneously unless future regulation addresses the obvious market imperfections that would ensue. For this reason, even should one accept the strongly conservative perspective of AI as primarily a tool in the artists' hands (see, e.g., Hertzmann, 2018), this might do little to affirm the autonomy of the artists themselves. Indeed, although it might not yet be the case that 'human art is close to total control by corporations' as Hoel (2021) suggests, the author is nevertheless likely to be correct in the longer perspective. This is particularly the case given that due to the complexity and the expense necessary to create large-scale creative AI agents, only the major players in the market would be able to afford the creation of AI-based generative systems.

Transformations in the creative industries may be, however, not only a coup from above but also a more grassroots move, whereby generative AI removes the skills and knowledge barrier that has traditionally been necessary for major creative endeavours, thereby democratising the production of creative artefacts. This, of course, would only further increase competition and further fragment audience attention but will also likely result in new styles and genres while also extending the current prosumer culture into the artistic domain (Bown, 2021, p. 300). In either case, established incentivisation models intended to encourage humans to enter and remain within the creative domain are unlikely to remain effective in their function because the exclusivity and scarcity that once made this possible would no longer apply.

Bibliography

Alacovska, A. (2022). The wageless life of creative workers: Alternative economic practices, commoning and consumption work in cultural labour. *Sociology, 56*(4), 673–692.

Amoore, L. (2020). *Cloud ethics: Algorithms and the attributes of ourselves and others.* Duke University Press.

Anantrasirichai, N., & Bull, D. (2022). Artificial intelligence and the creative industries: A review. *Artificial Intelligence Review, 55*, 589–656.

Arriagada, L. (2020). CG-Art: Demystifying the anthropocentric bias of artistic creativity. *Connection Science, 32*(4), 398–405.

Atkinson, P., & Barker, R. (2023). AI and the social construction of creativity. Convergence: *The International Journal of Research into New Media Technologies, 29*(4), 1054–1069.

Been, W. Wijngaarden, Y., & Loots, E. (2023). Welcome to the inner circle? Earnings and inequality in the creative industries. *Cultural Trends.* https://doi.org/10.1080/09548963.2023.2181057.

Boden, M. (2012). *Creativity and art: Three roads to surprise.* Oxford University Press.

Boden, M. (2016). *AI: Its nature and future.* Oxford University Press.

Bolojan, D. (2022). Creative AI: Augmenting design potency. *Architectural Design, 92*(3), 22–27.

Bown, O. (2021). *Beyond the creative species: Making machines that make art and music.* The MIT Press.

Brainard, L. (2023). The curious case of uncurious creation. *Inquiry.* https://doi.org/10.1080/0020174X.2023.2261503.

Broeckmann, A. (2019). The machine artist as myth. *Arts, 8*, 1–10.

Cacciatore, S., & Panozzo, F. (2022). Strategic mapping of cultural and creative industries: The case of the veneto region. *Creative Industries Journal.* https://doi.org/10.1080/17510694.2022.2026059.

Crespo, S., & McCormick, F. (2022). Augmenting digital nature: Generative art as a constructive feedback loop. *Architectural Design, 92*(3), 54–59.

Davenport, T. H., & Mittal, N. (2022, November 14). How generative AI is changing creative work. *Harvard Business Review.* https://hbr.org/2022/11/how-generative-ai-is-changing-creative-work.

De Cremer, D., Bianzino, N. M., & Falk, B. (2023, April 13). How generative AI could disrupt creative work. *Harvard Business Review.* https://hbr.org/2023/04/how-generative-ai-could-disrupt-creative-work.

Degli Eposti, M., Lagioia, F., & Sartor, G. (2020). The use of copyrighted works by AI systems: Art works in the data mill. *European Journal of Risk Regulation, 11*, 51–69.

Dignam, A. (2020). Artificial intelligence, tech corporate governance and the public interest regulatory response. *Cambridge Journal of Regions, Economy and* Society, *13*, 37–54.

Dornis, T. W. (2020). Artificial creativity: Emergent works and the void in current copyright doctrine. *Yale Journal of Law & Technology, 22,* 1–60.

Drott, E. (2021). Copyright, compensation, and commons in the music AI industry. *Creative Industries Journal, 14*(2), 190–207.

Du Sautoy, M. (2020). *The creativity code: How AI is learning to write, paint and think.* 4th Estate.

Eisikovits, N., & Stubbs, A. (2023, January 12). ChatGPT, DALL-E and the collapse of the creative process. *The Conversation.* https://theconversation.com/chatgpt-dall-e-2-and-the-collapse-of-the-creative-process-196461.

Elgammal, A. (2020, May 27). The Robot Artists aren't coming. *The New York Times.* www.nytimes.com/2020/05/27/opinion/artificial-intelligence-art.html.

Fergus, J. (2020). Spotify could soon relace real artists with AI music. *Input.* www.inputmag.com/tech/spotify-could-soon-replace-real-artists-with-ai-music.

Gohoungodji, P., & Amara, N. (2023). Art of innovating in the arts: Definitions, determinants, and mode of innovation in creative industries, a systematic review. *Review of Managerial Science, 17,* 2685–2725.

Gonzalez-Cristiano, A., & Le Grand, N. (2023). Achieving a shared understanding in the creative industries: Freelancers' use of boundary objects in collaborative innovation projects. *Creative Industries Journal.* https://doi.org/10.1080/17510694.2023.2218656.

Haugsevje, Å. D. (2022). Justifying creative work: Norwegian business support and the conflicting narratives of creative industries. *Cultural Trends.* https://doi.org/10.1080/09548963.2022.2126747.

Heaven, W. D. (2022, December 16). Generative AI is changing everything. But what's left when the hype is gone? *MIT Technology Review.* www.technologyreview.com/2022/12/16/1065005/generative-ai-revolution-art/.

Helberger, N., & Diakopoulos, N. (2023). ChatGPT and the AI act. *Internet Policy Review, 12*(1), 1–6.

Henriksen, D., Creely, E., & Mehta, R. (2022). Rethinking the politics of creativity: Posthumanism, indigeneity, and creativity beyond the western anthropocene. *Qualitative Inquiry, 28*(5), 465–475.

Hertzmann, A. (2018). Can computers create art? *Arts, 7,* 1–25.

Hoel, E. (2021, September 8). Big tech is replacing human artists with AI. *The Intrinsic Perspective.* https://erikhoel.substack.com/p/big-tech-is-replacing-human-artists.

Kalpokas, I. (2023). Work of art in the age of its AI reproduction. *Philosophy & Social Criticism.* https://doi.org/10.1177/01914537231184490.

Kelly, K. (2022, November 17). Picture limitless creativity at your fingertips. *Wired.* www.wired.com/story/picture-limitless-creativity-ai-image-generators/.

Kelly, R. (2023). Re-politicising the future of work: Automation anxieties, universal basic income, and the end of techno-optimism. *Journal of Sociology, 59*(4), 828–843.

Khlystova, O., & Kalyuzhnova, Y. (2023). The impact of the creative industries and digitalization on regional resilience and productive entrepreneurship. *The Journal of Technology Transfer.* https://doi.org/10.1007/s10961-023-10020-2.

Kinsella, E. (2021, August 2). Artificial intelligence may have cracked the code to creating low-priced works on canvas. *Artnet*. https://news.artnet.com/market/artifly-artificial-intelligence-art-1994150.

Kulp, P. (2020, November 25). This creative tech platform is selling AI-generated art for the holidays. *Adweek*. www.adweek.com/creativity/playform-artificial-intelligence-generated-art-holiday-pop-up-shop/.

Lee, H.-K. (2022). Rethinking creativity: Creative industries, AI and everyday creativity. *Media, Culture & Society, 44*(3), 601–612.

Lim, D. (2018). AI & IP: Innovation creativity in an age of accelerated change. *Akron Law Review, 52*(3), 813–876.

Manovich, L. (2022). AI & myths of creativity. *Architectural Design, 92*(3), 60–65.

Marčeta, P., Been, W., & Keune, M. (2023). Turning postmaterialism on its head: Self-expression, autonomy and precarity at work in the creative industries. *Cultural Trends*. https://doi.org/10.1080/09548963.2023.2241414.

Mazzone, M., & Elgammal, A. (2019). Art, creativity, and the potential of artificial intelligence. *Arts, 8*(1), 1–9.

Messingschlager, T. V., & Appel, M. (2023). Mind ascribed to AI and the appreciation of AI-generated art. *New Media & Society*. https://doi.org/10.1177/14614448231200248.

Millet, K., et al. (2023). Defending humankind: Anthropocentric bias in the appreciation of AI art. *Computers in Human Behavior, 143*, 1–9.

Morreale, F. (2021). Where does the buck stop? Ethical and political issues with AI in music creation. *Transactions of the International Society for Music Information Retrieval, 4*(1), 105–113.

Moruzzi, C. (2021). Measuring creativity: An account of natural and artificial creativity. *European Journal for Philosophy of Science, 11*(1), 1–20.

Naqvi, Z. (2020). Artificial intelligence, copyright, and copyright infringement. *Marquette Intellectual Property Law Review, 24*(1), 15–52.

Natale, S. (2022). The lovelace effect: Perceptions of creativity in machines. *New Media & Society*. https://doi.org/10.1177/14614448221077278.

Newton, A., & Dhole, K. (2023). Is AI art another industrial revolution in the making? *arXiv*. https://arxiv.org/abs/2301.05133.

Nolan, B. (2022, October 17). Artists say AI image generators are copying their style to make thousands of new images – and it's completely out of their control. *Business Insider*. www.businessinsider.com/ai-image-generators-artists-copying-style-thousands-images-2022-10.

Nowotny, H. (2022). *In AI we trust: Power, Illusion and control of predictive algorithms*. Polity Press.

O'Brien, A., & Arnold, S. (2022). Creative industries' new entrants as equality, diversity and inclusion change agents? *Cultural Trends*. https://doi.org/10.1080/09548963.2022.2141100.

O'Meara, J., & Murphy, C. (2023). Aberrant AI creations: Co-creating surrealist body horror using the DALL-E mini text-to-image generator. *Convergence: The International Journal of Research into New Media Technologies, 29*(4), 1070–1096.

Patrickson, B. (2021). What Do Blockchain Technologies Imply for Digital Creative Industries? *Creativity and Innovation Management, 30*(3), 585–595.

Papadimitriou, A., Mylonas, N., & Frangakis, C. (2022). Investigating women entrepreneurs in creative industries: Critical determinants for venture performance. *Creative Industries Journal*. https://doi.org/10.1080/17510694.2022.2077575.

Paris, T., & Mahmoud-Jouini, S. B. (2019). The process of creation in creative industries. *Creativity and Innovation Management, 28*(3), 403–419.

Peukert, C. (2019). The next wave of digital technological change and the cultural industries. *Journal of Cultural Economics, 43*, 189–210.

Potts, J. (2023). *The near-death of the author: Creativity in the internet age.* The University of Toronto Press.

Ramalho, A. (2022). *Intellectual Property Protection for AI-Generated Creations: Europe, the United States, Australia and Japan.* London and New York: Routledge.

Sætra, H. S. (2023). Generative AI: Here to stay, but for good? *Technology in Society, 75*, 1–5.

Shtefan, A. (2021). Creativity and artificial intelligence: A view from the perspective of copyright. *Journal of Intellectual Property Law & Practice, 16*(7), 720–728.

Sigurdardottir, M. S., & Candi, M. (2019). Growth strategies in creative industries. *Creativity and Innovation Management, 28*(3), 477–485.

Škiljić, A. (2021). When art meets technology or vice versa: Key challenges at the crossroads of AI-generated artworks and copyright law. *IIC – International Review of Intellectual Property and Competition Law, 52*, 1338–1369.

Stephenson, J. L. (2022). Artificial creativity: Beyond human, or beyond definition. *Transformations, 36*, 19–37.

Sun, D., Wang, H., & Xiong, J. (2023). Would you like to listen to my music, my friend? An experiment on AI musicians. *International Journal of Human-Computer Interaction.* https://doi.org/10.1080/10447318.2023.2181872.

Svedman, M. (2020). Artificial creativity: A case against copyright for AI-created visual artwork. *IP Theory, 9*(4), 1–22.

Szakálné Kanó, I., Vas, Z., & Klasová, S. (2023). Emerging synergies in innovation systems: Creative industries in Central Europe. *Journal of the Knowledge Economy, 14*, 450–471.

Tennakoon, T. (2022, December 17). AI art: Death of creative industry or its savior? *VentureBeat.* https://venturebeat.com/ai/ai-art-death-of-creative-industry-or-its-savior/.

Tigre Moura, F., Castrucci, C., & Hindley, C. (2023). Artificial intelligence creates art? An experimental investigation of value and creativity perceptions. *Journal of Creative Behavior.* https://doi.org/10.1002/jocb.600.

Velthuis, O. (2013). Art markets. In R. Towse (Ed.), *A handbook of cultural economics* (2nd ed., pp. 33–42). Edward Elgar.

Volpicelli, G. (2023). The new luddites: AI comes for the creative class. *Politico.* www.politico.eu/article/artificial-intelligence-technology-art-regulation-copyright/.

Walzer, D. (2023). Towards an understanding of creativity in independent music production. *Creative Industries Journal, 16*(1), 42–55.

Wingström, R., Hautala, J., & Lundman, R. (2022). Redefining creativity in the era of AI? Perspectives of computer scientists and new media artists. *Creativity Research Journal.* https://doi.org/10.1080/10400419.2022.2107 850.

Wohl, H. (2021). Innovation and creativity in creative industries. *Sociology Compass, 16*(2), 1–11.

Zatarain, J. M. N. (2017). The role of automated technology in the creation of copyright works: The challenges of artificial intelligence. *International Review of Law, Computers & Technology, 31*(1), 91–104.

Zeilinger, M. (2021). *Tactical Entanglements: AI Art, Creative Agency, and the Limits of Intellectual Property.* Lüneburg: Meson Press.

Zhao, Z., & Zhang, L. (2023). Design of artificial intelligence cultural creative industry based on machine learning. *Soft Computing.* https://doi.org/10.1007/s00500-023-08693-w.

3 Human Author vs AI

Can Copyright Still Protect Human Authors?

Copyright can be seen as 'critically important to a healthy culture' as it creates 'incentives to produce great new works that otherwise would not be produced' (Lessig, 2008, p. xvi). After all, a creative work both produces a positive externality (a cultural improvement) *and* is a public good: it can be consumed multiple times by multiple people without being depleted, and access to it can hardly be restricted (Lessig, 2008, p. 189). For this reason, copyright is typically presented as 'a policy bargain whereby exclusive rights and monopolies are granted as a reward to intellectual labour and investments in order to incentivise labour and creativity' (Noto La Diega, 2023, p. 275). Simultaneously, however, questions are being asked as to whether monetary incentives are the sole incentives: indeed, the presence of abundant, freely available content (particularly in the digital space) seems to indicate that there is a much broader variety of motivations and incentives behind creativity (Lessig, 2008, p. 291) – or perhaps there is even some inner compulsion to create, given the numerous cases of authors who continued to create despite living in poverty (Mammen & Richey, 2020). Nevertheless, the argument presented here is twofold: first, building on the central premise of copyright, the creation of artistic works benefits society (which seems to be uncontroversial even among the critically minded); second, although there are individuals who create despite the absence of remuneration, the lack of financial incentives produces a suboptimal situation whereby authors are discouraged from remaining in or embarking on creative careers, therefore precluding society from utilising its own creative potential.

Generally, there seems to be, in the words of Cohen (2007, p. 1156), a 'broader agreement on the importance of identifying a small set of first principles . . . from which a normatively compelling framework for copyright can then be derived in relatively neutral fashion'. As will be shown later, even the critical approaches to copyright that aim to demonstrate the false neutrality of the current regime do so by assuming their own standpoint to be neutral and objective. Here, as shown in the following, the why and how questions of copyright continue to cause the greatest controversy, while the what and the who questions (still) attract a much broader agreement. To define the object of

DOI: 10.4324/9781003464976-3

copyright protection (the what), one needs to turn to Article 2(1) of the Berne Convention, which directs the focus on 'literary and artistic works' and the requirement for fixation. It is also clear from Articles 2 to 6 of the Convention that the author of such works (the who) must have been a natural person (a human) (for a discussion, see, e.g., European Commission, 2020, p. 68; Yılmaztekin, 2023, pp. 80–81). Nevertheless, it can be postulated that generative AI capacities threaten these underlying assumptions behind copyright law, which means that 'protecting the personality of authors, enabling creative works to be duly rewarded, and stimulating creativity' can no longer be taken for granted, if they ever were (Degli Eposti et al., 2020, p. 68). Hence, the aim of this chapter is to dissect the key controversies pertaining to these crucial questions of copyright.

3.1 Outlining the Main Theories of Copyright

This section provides an overview of the main theoretical approaches to copyright (by effectively dealing with the why and how questions). These perspectives are identified as follows: utilitarian, rights-based (Lockean and Kantian/Hegelian), law and economics, and critical. Of course, it is impossible to do justice to the full complexities of and internal rivalries within each school of thought (and this is not the aim). Likewise, the scope of this overview is limited both thematically and geographically. Nevertheless, this section lays the groundwork for the subsequent discussion of copyright's functioning as an incentivisation tool for human authors rather than engaging in a full-scale debate on copyright theory.

To begin with, from a utilitarian point of view (which for the most part, underpins the US copyright doctrine), the provision of incentives to create and disseminate novel works is seen as a means for promoting general societal welfare (see, e.g., Fisher, 2001; Ramalho, 2022, p. 20). Copyright thus does not pertain to some inherent value of the work and does not even have the author's interests as its primary consideration (and, therefore, it is not the natural right of the author). Instead, societal benefit and progress constitute the primary concerns: since the creation of new works benefits society, it must be encouraged and incentivised so that societal good is maximised (; Ramalho, 2022, p. 20). Hence, although monopolies are generally seen as incompatible with societal good, the creation of monopoly entitlements in the narrow domain of creativity and for only a limited period of time is seen as both a necessary and a beneficial trade-off that enables the author to recoup their material and temporal investments; however, rights that cannot be demonstrated to reasonably contribute to such recouping or those that would diminish societal welfare cannot be granted – after all, according to this view, there are no natural rights that belong to the author (for a discussion, see Senftleben & Buijtelaar, 2020, p. 13). Accordingly, the key question to be answered to determine the utilitarian outlook towards the protection of AI output is whether there is something special about *human* creativity regarding the societal good that justifies the status difference. Given the dominance of the anthropocentric accounts of creativity already outlined in this book, it comes as no surprise that the prevailing answer is in the affirmative.

Rights-based approaches, meanwhile, consider copyright from the opposite direction. Here, copyright is the author's natural right, which is not created but merely recognised by copyright law (Ramalho, 2022, p. 21). The first of the rights-based approaches is the labour theory that originates from the writings of John Locke. Following the Lockean approach, although the resources necessary to create or otherwise produce something may be the common property of all, it is by mixing them with one's own labour that a person acquires the right to property that subsequently has to be accepted by all or, in the specific case of artistic creation, the author is taken to have mingled their 'personal creativity with the raw material of pre-existing sources of inspiration in the cultural landscape' (Senftleben & Buijtelaar, 2020, p. 12; see also Fisher, 2001; Ramalho, 2022, p. 21). Therefore, it is the expenditure and purposeful application of (in this case – creative) labour that gives rise to private property (Merges, 2011, p. 15). In the context of copyright, ideas or culture and tradition are common and cannot be owned, but the application of intellectual labour to turn such shared resources into a tangible work generates ownership as a reward for such labour (Ramalho, 2022, p. 22) – an entitlement that is not created by but instead precedes law, with the law simply acknowledging an established fact (Senftleben & Buijtelaar, 2020). Notably, the Lockean approach avoids the need to aggrandise the author – effectively, graft and investment give rise to property of whatever kind and regardless of other arrangements (Mayer-Schönberger, 2005, p. 5). In this case, it is immaterial whether and the extent to which the resulting work contributes to societal progress – ownership is simply a matter of production (which differs from the more strictly utilitarian approaches that emphasise societal benefit). This production, however, must be of a specific kind: it is not simply a matter of *adding* labour as merely yet another ingredient among the building blocks that the author already encounters in the world but instead 'the transformation of the preexisting thing by the expenditure of labor', and it is this transformative aspect that truly justifies claiming property rights (Merges, 2011, p. 15; see also Mayer-Schönberger, 2005, pp. 4–5). Of course, as AI cannot mix its own purposeful labour with cultural sources of inspiration (despite having access to the latter through machine learning), it is difficult to imagine a labour-based natural rights justification for the copyright protection of AI-generated content (Senftleben & Buijtelaar, 2020). By contrast, this theory views human entitlements not merely as incentives for further engagement in creative activities but also as that which already belongs to the human authors (i.e., a natural right).

Meanwhile, the second rights-based approach, personality theory, is mostly associated with Kant and Hegel and focuses not on labour as such but on the specificity of the relationship between the author and their work.

The work is seen as the expression and embodiment of the creator's personality; following Hegel in particular, since the free manifestation of the author's personality reveals itself in the work, alienation of the author from their work would also directly imply alienation from their own personality and being (Ramalho, 2022, p. 23). There is a clear link established between the author and the work that in itself suffices for an entitlement of the author to hold production and dissemination rights (Svedman, 2020, p. 12). For Kant, notably, there is an inextricable relationship among creativity, ownership, and freedom: specifically, the power and ability to shape external objects and imprinting oneself onto them (Merges, 2011, p. 17). Likewise, the Kantian approach presupposes a direct link among the author, the work, and the audience: effectively, the author communicates with the audience through the work, and it is the integrity of this link through which the author's personality interacts with that of a given audience member that merits protection (Mayer-Schönberger, 2005, p. 6). Since AI nether has nor is likely to have (at least in the foreseeable future) a personality to express through artistic creation and is incapable of forming a special bond with its own output, personality theory is even less likely than the previously discussed theories to support claims to AI authorship and the copyrightability of AI-generated content.

From a law and economics perspective, although creative efforts necessitate the expenditure of significant time and effort (hence, the creators bear a notable cost), the same cannot be said of those merely aiming to copy a work; copyright (and intellectual property (IP) more broadly) is thus claimed to be necessary to ensure that creators get a return on their investment or else the inability to do so would act as a deterrent for current and future artists (Fisher, 2001; see also Svedman, 2020). This, in turn, would harm not only the artists' own interests but also those of the public who have a demand for a continuous supply of creative output: therefore, if the artists suffer, then *by extension*, the public will also suffer (Dornis, 2020). At first glance, this view may seem to echo the utilitarian approach, but the focus here is different: the utilitarian justification of IP rights focuses on the societal good (artists positively contribute to society and have to be rewarded), while the law and economics approach is more individualistic (the author must be able to recover the costs inherent in the creative process). As the author is seen to be in an unfavourable position (the cost of creation is high, but the cost of copying is low; meanwhile, the goods created are essentially public and would therefore be underproduced in a completely free market), granting special monopoly rights is presented as a justifiable conclusion (Salzberger, 2011; Svedman, 2020). Crucially, contrary to land and other tangibles that are paradigmatic of property regimes, not the least due to their natural scarcity, there is no scarcity regarding informational and cultural goods, which means that their creation must be incentivised by introducing artificial scarcity through IP protection regimes (see, e.g., Salzberger, 2011). Posner (2005), meanwhile, introduces two further important points. First, arguing against the typical view that informational and cultural goods are non-rivalrous, he emphasises that the over-consumption of such goods leads to boredom and even disgust as audiences grow tired of encountering the same cultural artefacts over and over again. Second, the value creation of a cultural good does not cease at the moment of the good's own creation but instead has to be constantly maintained and increased through promotion and other means. In both cases, IP rights are seen as necessary to both prevent overuse and help recuperate not just creation but also ongoing value maintenance costs (Posner, 2005, p. 61). Regarding generative AI, notably, it is indeed expensive to create an AI model, while the generation of every particular expression is relatively cheap – in fact, the price is not much different from that of copying (arguably, the environmental impact may significantly differ between copying and generation), which again potentially undermines the argument for copyrightability (for a more extensive discussion, see Svedman, 2020, p. 14).

Elsewhere, critical studies of law and economics emphasise how IP rights constitute merely one more means that capitalism uses to enclose what would otherwise be the commons in order to exploit it for exclusive profit (Noto La Diega, 2023, p. 275). Although most other approaches (particularly the Lockean and law and economics perspectives) focus on the ways in which cultural artefacts are like or can be made to be more like physical property (and are thus enclosed and excluded from public consumption), critical approaches adopt the opposite view and focus on the immateriality and, therefore, openness of culture and knowledge (see, e.g., Mayer-Schönberger, 2005, p. 9; Mathew, 2021). Instead of concentrating on universal rights or enduring societal interests, critical approaches do exactly the opposite: they aim to demonstrate the temporal and contingent nature of what we tend to understand as the need to protect authorial works (Striphas & McLeod, 2006, p. 137; Mathew 2021, p. 116). Such approaches tend to be based on the central role of power relations in shaping legal regulation in the interests of those at the top of the political and economic hierarchy (see, e.g., Mayer-Schönberger, 2005, p. 6; Mathew, 2021, p. 116). Thus, copyright law is seen as an essentially conservative device to protect cultural incumbents: it stifles competition and enforces dominant (often gendered and racialised) modes of knowledge as uniquely valuable, thus conjoining knowledge/culture with political and economic power so that they become impossible to disentangle from one another (Tehranian, 2012, p. 1237; Craig, 2019; Mathew, 2021, pp. 116–117). In this way, control over knowledge and culture is simultaneously posited as a manifestation and a source of power; it entrenches particularistic interests and normative accounts of life and ultimately renders them seemingly natural and beyond contestation (Zhi, 2021, p. 304; see also Craig, 2019; Mathew, 2021). The very figure of the author (as engaged in creation as opposed to mere making or crafting) can thus be seen as a means of patriarchal exclusion that subsequently transcends into colonial (and arguably, post-colonial) exclusion (Mathew, 2021, pp. 118–119). These are certainly valid lines of critique, and they also pertain to the critique of dualist thinking and the seemingly blanket notion of *anthropos* stated earlier in this book. Likewise, the continued strengthening of copyright protection is seen as further proof of incumbents enforcing their interests through the law (see, e.g., Mayer-Schönberger, 2005, p. 8). In light of this, critical copyright scholars argue for the need to challenge not only existing copyright laws and their actual or perceived excesses but also the structures of power upon which they are premised by, for example, subverting, undermining, or routinely bypassing regulation (Striphas & McLeod, 2006, p. 130). The outcome is therefore a drive towards the 'revitalization of the public domain as a feminist decolonial enterprise' (Mathew, 2021, p. 116) so that the inclusivity of culture is ensured. Regarding AI, although the expansion of creativity and the drive towards eroding the strict boundaries of copyright protection are factors favourable to the inclusion of AI creativity, the corporate character of generative AI and its potential to further marginalise human authors would likely sit uneasily with critical scholars.

Some critical scholars (see, notably, Mathew, 2021) criticise the incentive-based approach towards IP protection as ahistorical, and they claim that it only represents a contingent and Western-specific way of thinking and of economic and social organisation (i.e., capitalism), whereas other cultures used to have (and often continue to have) vastly different interpretations of how knowledge and cultural artefacts come about. Certainly, arguing against this means contradicting the obvious. Nevertheless, this critical argument does not extend contingency far enough as it ignores is own situatedness, that is, the historical contingencies of past and present alternatives as if *their* forms of cultural and economic organisation were timeless and could be transplanted verbatim. Accordingly, one historical contingency is identified as exactly that, while another is presented as timeless and universal. Certainly, even in Western societies, the emergence of copyright was preceded by alternative conceptions of authorship and remuneration (as briefly outlined in the subsequent chapter). However, the radical transformation or even abolition of copyright and other forms of author remuneration and the embrace of an alternative system would require a corresponding societal and economic transformation. As it is not the aim if this book to consider the relative merits of economic systems and/or propose economic reforms beyond the incentivisation of human creativity, the need for remuneration is assumed to hold despite the recognition of some merits of the critical argument.

Overall, then, the intrinsic drive to create *and* the necessity to survive in the current economic system should be seen as coexistent: if economic rewards are not put in place, then individual creative drives may need to be put aside so that individuals can earn a living. However, of course, without individual-level creative drives and endeavours, there would be nothing to incentivise in the first place. Hence, incentivisation vs self-determination might as well be a false dichotomy; as Cohen (2007, p. 1155) puts it, 'the question whether creativity is produced largely from within or stimulated predominantly from without is a good question only if the answer must be one or the other', and there is no empirical quality as to their zero-sum nature. Even if greater openness is postulated as necessary for cultural innovation, it is also the case that 'copyright is a means of creating economic fixity, and thus predictability, in the organization of cultural production' (Cohen, 2007, p. 1195). Simultaneously, however, it is also important that 'copyright's goal of creating economic fixity must accommodate its mission to foster cultural play' (Cohen, 2007, p. 1196), and this normative debate plays out in various forms in the third part of this chapter.

3.2   Copyright Protection: The EU, the US, and Beyond

This section discusses the existing requirements of copyright protection in the EU, the US, and other selected jurisdictions and particularly focuses on the what (the work) and the who (the author) questions, because they are seen as key to understanding the position of the aforementioned legal regimes vis-à-vis the protection of AI-generated output. To make the point clear, at the heart of the argument pertaining to the debates on AI and copyright is not the quality of AI-generated output but its complicated relationship vis-à-vis the human. As Bonadio and McDonagh (2020, p. 1) claim, with AI-generated artwork or other ostensibly creative content, '[i]f such musical, literary and artistic expressions were created by humans, no one would object to them being considered as copyright works'. Therefore, it is the anthropocentric nature of copyright law that tends to largely disqualify AI-generated output from copyright considerations. Even if the law as it is can be criticised for focusing 'only on what was relevant in the past, namely the human authors behind the creative process' (Yanisky-Ravid & Velez-Hernandez, 2018, p. 14), this position is nevertheless very strongly entrenched, as shown in the later discussion of regulatory frameworks.

The anthropocentric nature of copyright is also enshrined in international human rights documents (see, notably, Universal Declaration of Human Rights (UDHR) Art. 27; International Covenant on Economic, Social and Cultural Rights (ICESCR) Art. 15) that stipulate the right of 'everyone' to reap the benefits of their creative endeavours. As Bonadio and McDonagh (2020, p. 3) note, the word 'everyone' can be taken to imply human exclusivity. Likewise, the Berne Convention, particularly Article 2(1) that features the term 'original works' as a requirement for protection, is traditionally understood as foregrounding a human-centric approach because original creativity (as opposed to data-based generation) is typically seen as exclusive to humans (see, e.g., Miernicki & Ng, 2021; Spindler, 2022). Thus, it is not surprising that AI-generated content largely falls outside copyright protection.

To begin with the EU, due to the prevalence of the moral rights and natural justice focus in the European approach to copyright, the copyrightability of AI-generated output here is unlikely (Canlas, 2020). As asserted by de Cock

Buning (2016, p. 315), the standard presumption under European law is that 'when the one that is the creator of the work is incapable of *human* creativity, it is most probably not capable of creating copyrightable works'. Notably, specific references in the Copyright Directive (2019/790) are made to 'author' and 'work', which are generally assumed to imply the need for a human (Miernicki & Ng, 2021). Moreover, as per the Software Directive (Art. 1(3)) and the Database Directive (Art. 3), the requirement for originality is stipulated in terms of the object to be protected being 'an author's own intellectual creation', and this requirement is extended to all copyrightable work by the CJEU in *Infopaq* (for a discussion, see Senftleben & Buijtelaar, 2020), leaving non-human entities outside the category of author (see, e.g., Pila & Torremans, 2019, p. 272; Yılmaztekin, 2023, p. 110).

The Court of Justice of the European Union's (CJEU) rulings also tend to follow the Berne Convention, specifically, Art. 2(1), because the Convention itself has been integrated into the EU's legal framework via the Agreement on Trade-Related Aspects of Intellectual Property Rights (TRIPS Agreement) and the World Intellectual Property Organization (WIPO) Copyright Treaty (Hugenholtz & Quintais, 2021, p. 1193; Ramalho, 2022, p. 25; Yılmaztekin, 2023, pp. 81–82), albeit perhaps in an open-ended manner and leaving room for broader conceptions of 'work' (Rosati, 2019, pp. 92–93). This reference to external sources is to be expected due to the still notable lack of harmonisation and lack of a clear definition of both 'author' and 'work' in existing EU legislation (Yılmaztekin, 2023, p. 84). Despite the Berne Convention omitting the definition of author, a *human* author is clearly inferred (Hugenholtz & Quintais, 2021, p. 1195; Ramalho, 2022, pp. 30–31). Likewise, the bar seems to be raised sufficiently by the CJEU so that only humans can qualify. This is particularly evident in the requirement for a creative touch as an expression of the author's personality, where '[b]y making those various choices, the author of a portrait photograph can stamp the work created with their "personal touch"' (the CJEU in *Painer*, para 92; see also *Football Dataco*, para 38); similarly, in *Cofemel* (para 30), the Court further elaborates that 'if a subject matter is to be capable of being regarded as original, it is both necessary and sufficient that the subject matter reflects the personality of its author, as an expression of his free and creative choices' (for a discussion, see, e.g., Pila and Torremans, 2019, pp. 260–261; Hugenholtz & Quintais, 2021, p. 1195). Therefore, for something to be protected, it must be 'the author's own intellectual creation', namely, original, as per Recital 17 of the Term Directive, and a work 'is to be considered original if it is the author's own intellectual creation reflecting his personality' (see also the CJEU in *Cofemel*, para 29; *Infopaq*, para 48; *Levola Hengelo*, para 36; *Painer*, para 95); it must also bear the author's 'personal touch' (*Painer*, para 92), display a manifestation of the author's 'free and creative choices' (*Football Dataco*, para 38), and be given specific expression by the author (*Brompton Bicycle*, para 22) (for a more extensive discussion, see, e.g., Yılmaztekin, 2023, pp. 99–101).

In effect, then, '[c]reative abilities – as a quality inherent to the author – must be put to good use when he or she is producing the work' (Ramalho, 2022, p. 28). In fact, as Hugenholtz and Quintais (2021) observe, in the EU, the *process* of creating a work is more important than the ultimate *expression* (as long as there *is* an intentionally selected expression). Hence, without personal authorial input within the creative process, no output counts. Consequently, it is the specific relationship between the work and its author, expressed in terms that are, at least for now, applicable only to humans, that gives rise to protection and not, for example, the quality of the end result: as the CJEU emphasises in *Cofemel* (para 54), the mere fact that something 'may generate an aesthetic effect' is insufficient. Consequently, even if generative AI models are (or will become) capable of producing output of great aesthetic quality, they still fall below the threshold of EU copyright law. Moreover, as also pointed out by Hugenholtz and Quintais, 2021, p. 1197), the return on investment argument, which is sometimes used by the proponents of awarding copyright protection to AI-generated output, does not apply here because mere investments of resources, be they monetary, skill, or labour resources, do not suffice (see *Football Dataco*, para 42; *Funke Medien*, para 23).

However, it is also important to consider that the mere creative combination of pre-existing ideas *can* suffice to satisfy the originality criterion (see, e.g., the CJEU in *Painer*, para 90–91), which does not discard data-based generation *in principle* (for a discussion, see also Spindler, 2022, pp. 260–261). Moreover, in cases when an AI tool makes a significant part of the arrangements, including those not originally anticipated by the initiator of the generation process, it might suffice that there is a human who 'has a general conception' prior to initiating the process and/or carries out significant post-generation editing (European Commission, 2020, pp. 75–80). It can therefore be argued that AI-generated content can be awarded copyright protection in the EU only as long as there is sufficient creative human input behind it (see also Hugenholtz & Quintais, 2021), that is, as long as generative AI is used as a tool for the expression of the *human* author in a way that is not dissimilar to a camera or editing software. Accordingly, 'there must be a link between the author's creativity and the work produced' (Ramalho, 2022, p. 28). As soon as generative AI models move beyond being mere tools and thus remove the need for human creative agency, copyright protection becomes unlikely. Notably, where technical considerations significantly limit the exercise of free and creative choices or where other similar constraints exist, the originality criterion would unlikely be fulfilled (see, e.g., *Brompton Bicycle*, para 24; *Cofemel*, para 31; *Football Dataco*, para 39). As indicated by Ramalho (2022, pp. 27–28), this might negatively affect the possibility of the protection of AI-generated content, especially should technical considerations and rules be interpreted as the code and model inherent to the AI tool. Therefore, although the what question remains ambiguous (AI generation does not preclude copyrightability in principle, and there are circumstances when AI-generated works could potentially be protected), the who question has a very straightforward answer: whatever the way in which the work is made, it must reflect the author's personality through their own free and creative choices. Consequently, when the AI model is more advanced and autonomous, the copyrightability of its output becomes less likely.

The copyright landscape also appears to be very similar in China. Particularly, two recent court cases illustrate the human-centricity of copyright. In *Beijing Film Law Firm v Beijing Baidu Netcom Science & Technology Co Ltd*, the Beijing Internet Court ruled that computer-generated work cannot be copyrightable, and authorship by a natural person is a prerequisite. Meanwhile, in *Shenzhen Tencent Computer System Co Ltd v Shanghai Yingxun Technology Co Ltd*, the court determined that there was sufficient human involvement in the generation of a work to make it copyrightable. Once again, the role of the human is central to determining if the output merits protection. Of course, the threshold is not particularly high: direct human creativity is not required, and mere involvement suffices; nevertheless, it is still clear that software cannot be 'the subject of creation' either (Wan & Lu, 2021, p. 9).

As for Japan, its Copyright Act in Article 2(1)(i) establishes a triple test: the work under consideration must be an original and creative expression of feelings or thoughts in the scientific, literary, musical, or artistic domains. Once again, creativity does not necessitate novelty but instead, the imprinting of an author's personality and expression of their own feelings and thoughts – in this sense, the representation of something ordinary or something that has been selected from only a limited number of choices cannot be considered creative (for a broader discussion, see Ramalho, 2022, pp. 47–48). In terms of authorship, Japan adheres to the author's rights approach similar to that in Europe (as evident from the need of an author's imprint); likewise, the focus on feelings and thoughts clearly implies that the author is expected to be a human (Ramalho, 2022, p. 48). Crucially, active human involvement in the creation process is necessary, which must go beyond the mere provision of materials or otherwise arranging the conditions for the process (Ramalho, 2022, p. 49). In turn, this suggests that AI-generated content cannot be awarded copyright protection in Japan.

In the US, section 102(a) of the Copyright Act purports that copyright protection extends to 'original works of authorship fixed in any tangible medium of expression, now known or later developed, from which they can be perceived, reproduced, or otherwise communicated, either directly or with the aid of a machine or device'. Hence, the originality and fixation elements are key. US case law on the subject can be dated to *Burrow-Giles Lithographic Co. v. Sarony* (1884), whereby a manifestation of the author's 'intellectual conception' was deemed to be necessary. Likewise, in *Feist*, mere industriousness was found to be insufficient, and at least *some* degree of creativity was deemed to be necessary to give rise to originality and, therefore, protectability, although this is typically seen as a requirement to take at least a marginal step beyond that which is merely borrowed, naturally existing, or completely predetermined by external requirements (see, e.g., Senftleben & Buijtelaar, 2020; Murray, 2023). Likewise, although the originality criterion is key, one should read it in a rather narrow sense: not necessarily as 'unique, clever, ingenious, or inventive' but simply as denoting that 'the work originates with the author and is not copied from another author's work' (Murray, 2023, p. 31; for relevant US case law, see also *Feist*). As for the author, it is clear that only humans can be the creators of copyrightable works (Ramalho, 2022, p. 35; see also e.g., *Community for Creative Non-Violence v. Reid*; *Naruto v. Slater*). Clearly, the figure of the author is central here because '[w]ithout authorship, the concept of works as being "original" or a "creation" has no meaning' (Murray, 2023, p. 31). Elsewhere, the wording is also quite clear: for example, in *Feist*, being 'founded in the creative powers of the mind' was deemed to be necessary, thus rather unequivocally implying a human creative agent. Moreover, as Senftleben and Buijtelaar (2020) observe, with the choice of words such as 'compilation', 'choice', or 'arrangement', the US Supreme Court has, since *Burrow-Giles Lithographic*, implied the need for *both* the end result and the actor producing it to be creative.

Narrowing the discussion down specifically to AI, particularly relevant is the Final Report of the National Commission on New Technological Uses of Copyrighted Works, which considers computers to be mere instruments at the hands of humans. Similarly, as stipulated in the *Compendium of US Copyright Office Practices* (Art. 306), the requirement for copyrightable works to be 'original intellectual conceptions of the author' means that 'the Office will refuse to register a claim if it determines that a human being did not create the work'. Therefore, as eloquently stated by Murray (2023, p. 32), 'the problem of generative art and copyright does not arise because the works are not original, or created, or fixed, or existing in a tangible medium' but instead because '[i]f successful, then the generative work lacks a human author'. Meanwhile, as explicitly formulated in the *Compendium*, 'to qualify as a work of "authorship" a work must be created by a human being. Works that do not satisfy this requirement are not copyrightable'; moreover, 'the Office will not register works produced by a machine or mere mechanical process that operates randomly or automatically without any creative input or intervention from a human author' (Art. 313.2). The human-specificity of the author is clear and manifests itself not only vis-à-vis machines but also in relation to non-human animals, as demonstrated in, for example, *Naruto v Slater* (otherwise known as the 'monkey selfie' case). Crucially, there have also been cases of the US Copyright Office refusing to grant copyright protection to AI-generated outputs, including a graphic novel (Escalante de Mattei, 2023) and a painting (Brittain, 2023). Likewise, should one attempt to draw a crude analogy between claims of divine (or other supernatural) authorship and AI authorship, then, following *Urantia Foundation v. Maaherra* and *Penguin Books v. New Christian Church of Full Endeavor*, protection should fall on the closest human who had enabled and maintained the expression of abstract ideas in a concrete form and medium rather than 'celestial voices' and other supernatural sources (see, e.g., Bonadio & McDonagh, 2020, p. 3; Ramalho, 2022, p. 36). Nevertheless, this human involvement must be substantial in some way and cannot be restricted to the mere provision of enabling conditions, as demonstrated in *Naruto*. Overall, it is thus clear that no copyright can persist under US law unless a proximate human contribution can be found, and this contribution must be substantial enough to intentionally and directly determine the substance of the resulting work (to this effect, see also Miernicki & Ng, 2021).

A somewhat different approach is found in the UK. Although it starts from the same premise that human involvement is necessary, the Copyright, Designs and Patents Act of 1988 allows for the copyrightability of a computer-generated work and stipulates in Section 9(3) that in such cases, 'the author shall be taken to be the person by whom the arrangements necessary for the creation of the work are undertaken'. That is, as in the jurisdictions mentioned earlier, the most proximate human author is sought. However, here, greater leniency regarding the nature of human contribution can be found, as arrangement-making does not necessitate having substantial control over the output or even a conception of the latter. In this way, the meaning of authorship is extended beyond the creation of the work and turned into a legal fiction for vesting rights in the subject who is actually capable of owning them – and an AI model, for example, cannot own them (for a more extensive commentary, see, e.g., Canlas, 2020, p. 1065). For some scholars (see, e.g., Guadamuz, 2017, 2021), such a model is preferable as it is said to balance the interests of users of generative AI tools (who rely on such systems being developed) and the developers themselves (who need incentives to carry on with their work). However, the lack of traceability and explainability of AI-generated output as machine learning models that proceeds through multiple instances of trial and error until output is generated (see, e.g., Ramalho, 2022, p. 12) puts the value and possibility of making the necessary arrangements into question. Moreover, it could be suggested that a wide application of this doctrine could lead to a concentration of (most likely corporate) ownership of copyright with AI-equipped actors being able to generate and hoard large amounts of protected content (see, e.g., Bonadio & McDonagh, 2020, p. 4).

Overall, as the law currently stands, the previously discussed jurisdictions require the centrality and inescapability of human authorship or at least human involvement for copyright protection to arise. Therefore, it must be emphasised that '[i]f a human author cannot be traced throughout the creative process . . . (or if one simply does not exist), the consequence is that the output generated by the AI system cannot be protected by copyright, being thus in the public domain' (Ramalho, 2022, p. 57). Indeed, perhaps without much of a stretch, one could assert that the anthropocentric conception of copyright, which is focused on *human* authorship and *human* creativity, constitutes a widespread principle, thereby leaving no room for the protection of AI output (for an overview, see, e.g., Zurth, 2021).

3.3 What Should Be Done?

Awarding protection to AI itself is, for now, out of the question because it does not have legal personality and, therefore, the capacity to have rights (see, e.g., Matulionyte & Lee, 2022). As long as AI is not recognised as having legal personhood and is consequently incapable of having any rights, including copyright, acknowledging machines as authors is highly unlikely (Bonadio & McDonagh, 2020, p. 7). Similarly, for Shtefan (2021, p. 726), only a human can be the owner of a copyright due to their agency not just in the creative process but also in decision-making, management, and responsibility-taking. Moreover, it can be claimed with little risk of controversy that since AI does not have its own agentic capacity, it does not need incentives to create and is therefore incapable of benefitting from the fruits of its own labour, contrary to human authors (Spindler, 2022, p. 269; see also Lauber-Rönsberg and Hetmank, 2019, p. 576; Paquette, 2021, p. 210; Ramalho, 2022, p. 62). Likewise, AI has no free will and does not generate out of an authentic creative impulse but only because it is instructed to do so; consequently, AI does not and cannot need incentives beyond such instruction (Canlas, 2020, p. 1077; Senftleben & Buijtelaar, 2020). Similarly, there cannot be said to be any investment in terms of time, money, or other material resources by AI and consequently, there is nothing for it to recuperate (Senftleben & Buijtelaar, 2020, p. 15). Hence, recognising AI authorship under copyright law is not justifiable under any of the main theoretical approaches to copyright law.

Likewise, arguments against copyright protection for AI-generated output are derived from the very nature of the creative process, as only human creativity is seen as independent and truly innovative. Making free and creative choices stemming from the author's personality and individual capacity in a goal-oriented process (the human way of creativity) is prioritised over AI's reproduction and rearrangement of patterns in the training data (see, e.g., Shtefan, 2021, p. 728; Ramalho, 2022, p. 62). If copyright is understood in terms of incentivising the creation of artistic works for the benefit of society as a whole (the utilitarian approach), then an argument can be made that awarding copyright protection to AI-generated content is nonsensical because AI cannot have inter-human sensibilities (Canlas, 2020, p. 1077). Moreover, should one approach the matter from a personality and rights perspectives (which is dominant in Continental Europe and Japan), AI, at least in the current stage of its development, cannot be seen as having a personality that can be imprinted on the content that it generates and therefore cannot have a special self-expressive relationship with such output (see, e.g., Ramalho, 2022, p. 62). AI simply lacks both the connection with the resulting work and self-expressive capacity (namely due to having no 'self' to be expressed) to merit special protection (Canlas, 2020, p. 1077).

Notably, the no-copyright approach also has the added convenience of not necessitating any change in the law by reaffirming copyright law's human-centricity and shifting the debate towards the nature and essence rather than the function and performance of the author; likewise, such a solution could, at least in theory, help preserve human incentives because of obstructing the monetisation of AI's output (Franceschelli & Musolesi, 2022, p. 10). In either case, it has been argued in the literature that a failure to retain human-centredness in copyright protection would undermine its very purpose (Paquette, 2021, p. 213). However, this lack of attractiveness of machine-generated works might cause unfair behaviour, such as a failure to disclose the actual mode of creation to deceive one's way into protectability (see, e.g., Bonadio & McDonagh, 2020; Franceschelli & Musolesi, 2022). Likewise, as Salami (2021, p. 135) asserts, 'it would amount to an economic loss if the creativity of AI systems is not exploited for commercial and economic growth'. Still, it can be argued that the efficiency of AI content generation is such that investment could be recuperated even in the case of marginal returns, thereby benefitting AI companies and challenging human artists.

If AI-generated outputs are deemed to be uncopyrightable, then the simplest solution might be to automatically consider them as belonging to the public domain; thus, such output would be rendered not dissimilar to 'things found in nature, such as music that the wind generates when it moves through wind chimes, or the sounds of a waterfall, or birds singing at dawn' (Bonadio & McDonagh, 2020, p. 11). Moreover, the public domain solution would help protect against AI-equipped actors, most likely large technology companies, from hoarding mass-produced copyrighted works and only further entrenching their dominance (Bonadio & McDonagh, 2020, p. 11). In addition, the public domain solution is seen as a means to protect human authors and the faculty of human creativity – potentially even human progress as such (Gervais, 2020).

Nevertheless, it must also be acknowledged that things found in nature and many other objects in the public domain do not necessitate investment: they simply exist regardless of human effort and input. AI-generated content, meanwhile, requires the development of underlying technology, which means that a restriction of monetisation options could jeopardize technological development (see, e.g., Guadamuz, 2017). No less importantly, as argued by Bonadio and McDonagh, the public domain solution 'would bring about an absurd result: a very simple and banal stick man sketched by a human hand in just a few seconds would be more worthy of protection than a sophisticated machine-created painting'. However, within the ambit of this book, there is an even more fundamental threat arising from AI-generated output: the abundance of such works in the public domain might crowd out human authors.

Potential buyers would choose the cheaper or free option even in the presence of a qualitatively better human-created one, thereby reducing incentives for human authors (Franceschelli & Musolesi, 2022, p. 10; Spindler, 2022, p. 268). As Lee (2022, p. 606) emphasises, when the gap is broader between (strong) human-centric protection and the (weak or non-existent) protection of AI-generated content, 'the more demand for AI creation we will observe'. This could be seen as a paradoxical effect of the status quo that focuses on human exclusivity in copyright protection.

An interesting argument is proposed by Lauber-Rönsberg & Hetmank (2019, p. 578): should AI-generated content remain unprotected, this would also destabilise the views on human creativity because 'if AI-"works" are perceived to be equivalent or even "better" than human works, but enjoy a lesser degree of protection', then the need to justify (and by extension, calls to obliterate) the copyright protection of human output would only grow. As Spindler (2022, p. 268) argues, the introduction of some form of protection for AI-generated outputs could potentially level the playing field to some extent by introducing scarcity (see also, e.g., Gervais, 2020; Senftleben & Buijtelaar, 2020). However, even if AI creations are taken to be copyrightable in some way, the sharp increase in copyrighted works on the market will drive down the price – particularly since it is difficult to foresee a corresponding spike in demand (see, e.g., Mammen & Richey, 2020). Simultaneously, as Picht and Thouvenin (2023) observe, the lack of legal protection might not necessarily mean a corresponding lack of means to introduce some form of artificial scarcity by technological means, such as watermarks or a blockchain-based proof of provenance.

There are also industry-focused arguments in favour of protecting AI-generated output. These arguments tend to invert the usual approach by concentrating not on artists' incentives to create new works but on human incentives to develop generative AI tools; hence, the removal or weakening of incentives for AI-generated tools is seen as slowing progress and leading to a suboptimal situation for the consumers who would be able to enjoy fewer new works than they otherwise could (Bisoyi, 2022, p. 383). Perhaps one of the most pronounced perspectives here is proposed by Lim (2018) who rejects the 'Luddite' view that AI-generated outputs should not be protected for the sake of maintaining incentives for human creators and presents this as 'destabilizing the very foundation of investment, risk-taking, and entrepreneurship that are seen to undergird the very notion of progress'. As the argument goes, '[i]t is futile for Luddites to fight over obsolete technologies and yesterday's jobs' (Lim, 2018, p. 827), including, for example, in the creative industries. To this effect, according to Lim (2018, p. 837), the law should be creator-agnostic and be concerned solely with progress: '[i]f the progress of creative output depends on incentivizing its creation, then it is incumbent on the law to find the proper vehicle to attribute the work's expressive value, whether that vehicle is the AI, a human, or a corporation'. Indeed, it might well be the case that 'investors would be reluctant to invest in the development of AI if they were unable to exclude third parties from using the outcome' (Lauber-Rönsberg & Hetmank, 2019, p. 576; see also Lim, 2018, p. 841). As Salami (2021, p. 135) claims, it is crucial to ensure 'that our laws develop and can support rather than inhibit technological advancements'. In this way, the protection of AI-generated works is seen as combined with a notion of progress (see also, e.g., Wang, 2023). Following this line of argument, only if 'the human innovators in the AI industry' are sufficiently incentivised to develop and bring to market new technologies, then one can expect 'the optimal number of AI applications and, accordingly, the optimal amount of emergent works' (Dornis, 2020, p. 35; see also Brown, 2018, p. 22). Similarly, for Brown (2018, p. 20), '[o]ffering copyright protection to computer-generated works would directly advance copyright's purpose of encouraging the production of original literary, artistic, and musical expression for the good of the public'. Since the goal of copyright is progress, and progress is to be measured by the number of works produced, it is claimed that incentivising the generation of AI outputs (particularly given the efficiency of AI tools) would then be seen as a clear vehicle of progress (Brown, 2018, p. 21). Although it is more easily compatible with the law and economics approach to copyright, this perspective lacks the evidence of AI-generated works' contribution to societal development needed for the utilitarian justification and does nothing to address personality-based arguments. Moreover, it is difficult to overlook the one-sidedness of this approach that unilaterally favours industry interests over human considerations.

One popular alternative proposal is to award copyright protection to the programmers/developers behind the AI model, and the reasoning is that the creators of the tool are the true cause of and the ones ultimately responsible for what it produces even if they had not foreseen any of the individual outputs (Canlas, 2020, pp. 1078–1079; see also Bonadio & McDonagh, 2020, p. 5). Others arrive at a similar conclusion through a more progressivist stance: as the autonomy of AI generators and the quality of their output increase to the extent that AI can be seen as not just quantitatively but also qualitatively outperforming humans, the case for protecting AI-generating output to reward the developers also becomes stronger (Bisoyi, 2022, p. 382). There are clear benefits of this approach, such as rewarding the true 'first mover' and incentivising technological development by remunerating programmers/developers for the results of their labour (Canlas, 2020, p. 1079). Likewise, it is, arguably, programmers who invest time and money into the creation of such tools, and they therefore need a return on their investment (Senftleben & Buijtelaar, 2020, p. 15). Moreover, this strategy clearly has the benefit of simplicity, certainty, and foreseeability as it removes the need for evaluating the relative importance of different parties' contributions: 'if you own the AI, you own its AI-generated outputs' (Matulionyte & Lee 2022, p. 30). Considerably, this can be seen as a concretisation of the previous argument for protectability and includes the same drawbacks, namely, one-sidedness and the ensuing disregard for human authors' interests.

A question also remains as to the incentives for end users who are thus deprived of ownership. For example, Naqvi (2020) argues that AI tools could be treated as consumer goods, thus by implication, treating the end user as author, which comes close to the UK model of making the necessary arrangements. However, although the UK model can accommodate anyone from programmers to end users, this proposal more specifically favours the one group that is involved in the generation process. Moreover, it has been claimed that if there is only very limited benefit to be derived by users, the demand for generative AI tools would drop and, in turn, reduce the incentives for programmers (Senftleben & Buijtelaar, 2020, p. 16). However, as Matulionyte and Lee (2022, p. 34) assert, in a free market, developers would be competing for end users and provide them with attractive ownership options, for example, through licencing (a similar prediction is also expressed by Senftleben & Buijtelaar, 2020). Such user-centricity, nevertheless, would be limited in oligopolistic markets where very few suppliers dominate a particular area (which is often characteristic of the technology industry), potentially leading to suboptimal outcomes for users. However, a question must again be raised as to whether such incentivisation satisfies the copyright rationale of serving societal good: if, as argued earlier, incentivising AI creativity might not fall under such a justification, it is difficult to imagine how doing so indirectly (by incentivising the creators or users of generators) would be any different.

An argument can also be put forward that there are simply too many parties contributing to the development of today's increasingly complex AI systems, rendering the identification of the main beneficiary of copyright impossible (Paquette, 2021, pp. 206–207). In fact, it should be uncontroversial to claim that there is hardly any direct causal link between the programmers and every *specific* generated content item (Svedman, 2020, p. 13). What exists is, at best, a *general* causal link between the programmers and the process of AI-enabled generation *as such*. Furthermore, as AI tools are typically protected themselves (such as by copyright or patent, depending on the circumstances and jurisdiction), awarding copyright also to the AI-generated content and designating the developers as copyright owners would amount to a double reward (Ramalho, 2022, p. 61). In addition, there is also the question of fairness, since although it is undeniable that without the creation of generative models there would be no generative artwork itself (a common argument *for* treating programmers as authors), it is far from certain who has had the most significant contribution in the emergence of a specific work, that is, the programmer or the user; therefore, if users have a large degree of freedom to determine their own choices, then leaving them out of the equation might be difficult to justify (Bonadio & McDonagh, 2020, p. 5). No less importantly, generative AI could not be trained if there were no human-created works in the first place.

The preceding discussion, however, does not include the only ways for copyright allocation. Notably, the US Copyright Act (see sections 101 and 201) provides the possibility for copyright to be owned by an entity that, by employing or commissioning the creator, becomes the substantial initiator of the creative process, while the creator is reduced to an agent of the entity in what is known as works made for hire; the premise is that it is the employer who creates the conditions for the work to come into being (Canlas, 2020, p. 1080; see also Lim, 2018; Bisoyi, 2022; Franceschelli & Musolesi, 2022; Ramalho, 2022, p. 38). In this way, an AI model would be treated as approximate to an employee, thereby precluding AI-generated works from falling into the public domain. After all, since no generative AI tool (as yet) possesses full creative autonomy and therefore has to be determined by somebody else, it could potentially be deemed to be that person's agent (Lim, 2018; Cedillo-Lazcano, 2020). As Lim (2018, p. 844) states, with the adoption of work-for-hire, '[t]he corporation provides a vehicle to exploit the rights and accept responsibility for liabilities, and a commercially expedient alternative to human authorship' (for a similar argument, see also Yanisky-Ravid, 2017). Nevertheless, this view is not beyond criticism. In particular, the treatment of AI in an employee-like way disregards the fact that AI lacks the capacity to enter into a contractual relationship or to have and assert the rights and benefits typically provided in an employment contract, thereby rendering the machine short of the status of an employee (see, e.g., Bonadio & McDonagh, 2020, p. 4; Ramalho, 2022, p. 39).

Moreover, the application of the work-for-hire doctrine to AI tools would reverse the very reasoning and purpose of the original doctrine: while its traditional version, in a way, retained an anthropocentric character (by using a legal fiction to attribute the creation of a work by a human to a non-human entity, i.e., the employer), here, a fiction would be used to attribute non-human authorship to a human or to another non-human in the case of a corporate 'employer' (Bonadio & McDonagh, 2020, p. 4). Additionally, Paquette (2021, p. 210) provides an equality-focused argument against work-for-hire: the price of AI models is such that only large corporations would be able to 'hire' them, leading to already rich and influential actors hoarding IP. No less important is that for the employer or commissioner of the work to own the copyright, the underlying work must be copyrightable in the first place, which brings us back to the human authorship requirement – unless this is fulfilled, there is nothing to transfer (Ramalho, 2022, p. 39). In the end, this approach would have further negative consequences to human authors, whereby the efficiency (and, therefore, lower marginal unit cost of a work) of AI tools means that 'hiring' machines would become more attractive than hiring a human artist for the same job (Paquette, 2021, p. 210).

Jung (2020, p. 1154), for example, claims that since AI tools are specifically designed to imitate human creativity, 'they produce creative works that are outside the control of the original programmer'. Likewise, due to the machine learning nature of AI models, they have the capacity to change and adapt to new data beyond the original anticipation of developers, thereby further diminishing potential claims to owning the copyright (Canlas, 2020,

p. 1081). Hence, Jung (2020) and Paquette (2021) propose moving beyond discussions about the copyrightability of AI-generated works and focusing on the monetisation of the underlying software, and they claim that this would still incentivise developers without the need to radically rethink copyright law. Nevertheless, for this model to work, *end users* need to have incentives to, for example, pay subscription fees to developers for the use of AI models, which necessitates some form of ownership of the end result. In a way, this is not too dissimilar from the UK model as the end user is ultimately the one who makes the decisions most proximate to the generation of the work, including the decision to start generating in the first place (Canlas, 2020, p. 1084).

Meanwhile, a separate group of proposals aims to solve the return on investment conundrum through alternative means, such as suggesting sui generis protection for AI-generated output, similar to the sui generis protection of databases. As per Article 1(2) of the Database Directive, a database is defined as 'a collection of independent works, data, or other materials arranged in a systematic and methodical way and individually accessible by electronic or other means'. An additional important factor is that there must have been substantial investment (either qualitatively or quantitatively) in the compilation of the database, either in monetary terms or in the form of time and energy (Database Directive, Article 7). However, as Spindler (2022, p. 264) indicates, the applicability of this framework would likely be limited, since the Directive focuses on *obtaining* existing data (see, e.g., *Fixtures Marketing* or *British Horseracing Board*), whereas generative AI models *produce* new data; likewise, although the individual summands of the database must be independent from one another and separable from the whole without losing their quality and essence (see, e.g., *Fixtures Marketing*), individual elements (words, pixels, sounds, etc.) in AI-generated content can only be meaningfully taken as a whole.

Therefore, it is clear that the copyright protection of AI-generated works cannot be derived from either the dominant theoretical approaches or the law as it is. However, notable voices within the academic community propose alternative takes on the copyrightability of AI-generated content, typically aiming to develop more industry-friendly argumentation. It was not the aim of this chapter to argue *for* a particular approach but instead to provide an overview of the different approaches to copyright protection of AI-generated works. From this angle, it appears unlikely that the interests and incentives for human authors can be effectively preserved through copyright law. If AI-generated works are seen as not meriting protection and belonging to the public domain, then this would leave human authors needing to compete against a tsunami of free or relatively cheap content. However, the opposite solution – awarding protection to AI-generated output – would not fare any better because the productivity of AI would simply drive down the value of copyrighted works due to an exponential growth in supply. Moreover, the industry-centric logic of such arguments implies a drive towards resource reallocation whereby technology companies would reap the largest benefits of creativity. Accordingly, additional options for human incentivisation should be sought.

Bibliography

Bisoyi, A. (2022). Ownership, liability, patentability, and creativity in artificial intelligence. *Information and Security Journal: A Global Perspective*, *31*(4), 377–386.

Bonadio, E., & McDonagh, L. (2020). *Artificial intelligence as producer and consumer of copyright works: Evaluating the consequences of algorithmic creativity* . https://papers.ssrn.com/sol3/papers.cfm?abstract_id=3617197.

Brittain, B. (2023, September 7). US copyright office denies protection for another AI-created image. *Reuters* . www.reuters.com/legal/litigation/us-copyright-office-denies-protection-another-ai-created-image-2023-09-06/.

Brown, N. I. (2018). Artificial authors: A case for copyright in computer-generated works. *Columbia Science and Technology Law Review*, *20*(1), 1–41.

Canlas, J. D. (2020). Solving copyright quandary: Proposing framework for assigning copyright to creative works made by AI. *Ateneo Law Journal*, *64*(3), 1045–1102.

Cedillo-Lazcano, I. (2020). AI©R. International review of law. *Computers & Technology*, *34*(2), 201–213.

Cohen, J. E. (2007). Creativity and culture in copyright theory. *University of California Davis Law Review*, *40*, 1151–1205.

Craig, C. J. (2019). Critical copyright law & the politics of 'IP'. In E. Christodoulidis, R. Dukes, & M. Goldoni (Eds.) *Research handbook on critical legal theory* (pp. 301–323). Edward Elgar.

de Cock Buning, M. (2016). Autonomous intelligent systems as creative agents under the EU framework for intellectual property. *European Journal of Risk Regulation*, *7*(2), 310–322.

Degli Eposti, M., Lagioia, F., & Sartor, G. (2020). The use of copyrighted works by AI Systems: Art works in the data mill. *European Journal of Risk Regulation*, *11*, 51–69.

Dornis, T. W. (2020). Artificial creativity: Emergent works and the void in current copyright doctrine. *Yale Journal of Law & Technology*, *22*, 1–60.

Escalante de Mattei, S. (2023, March 21). US Copyright Office : AI Generated Works Are Not Eligible for Copyright. *ARTnews*, https://www.artnews.com/art-news/news/ai-generator-art-text-us-copyright-policy-1234661683/.

European Commission. (2020). Trends and developments in artificial intelligence. *Challenges to the Intellectual Property Rights Framework: Final Report.* https://data.europa.eu/doi/10.2759/683128.

Fisher, W. (2001). Theories of intellectual property. In S. Munzer (Ed.), *New essays in the legal and political theory of property* (pp. 168–200). Cambridge University Press.

Franceschelli, G., & Musolesi, M. (2022). Copyright in generative deep learning. *Data & Policy, 4*, 1–18.

Gervais, D. J. (2020). The machine as author. *Iowa Law Review, 105*, 2053–5106.

Guadamuz, A. (2017). Artificial intelligence and copyright. *WIPO Magazine* . www.wipo.int/wipo_magazine/en/2017/05/article_0003.html.

Guadamuz, A. (2021). Do Androids Dream of Electric Copyright? Comparative Analysis of Originality in Artificial Intelligence Generated Works. I. J.-A. Lee, R. Hilty and K.-C. Liu (eds.). *Artificial intelligence and Intellectual Property*. Oxford and New York: Oxford University Press, pp. 147–176.

Hugenholtz, P. B., & Quintais, J. P. (2021). Copyright and artificial creation: Does EU copyright law protect AI-assisted output? *IIC – International Review of Intellectual Property and Competition Law, 52*, 1190–1216.

Jung, G. (2020). Do androids dream of copyright? Examining AI copyright ownership. *Berkeley Technology Law Journal, 35*(4), 1151–1178.

Lauber-Rönsberg, A., & Hetmank, S. (2019). The concept of authorship and inventorship under pressure: Does artificial intelligence shift paradigms? *Journal of Intellectual Property Law & Practice, 17*(7), 570–579.

Lee, H.-K. (2022). Rethinking creativity: Creative industries, AI and everyday creativity. *Media, Culture & Society, 44*(3), 601–612.

Lessig, L. (2008). *Remix: Making art and commerce thrive in the hybrid economy*. Bloomsbury Academic.

Lim, D. (2018). AI & IP: Innovation creativity in an age of accelerated change. *Akron Law Review, 52*(3), 813–876.

Mammen, C. E., & Richey, C. (2020). AI and IP: Are creativity and inventorship inherently human activities? *Florida International University Law Review, 14*, 275–292.

Mathew, S. (2021). A feminist manifesto of resistance against intellectual property regimes: Reclaiming the public domain as an open-access information commons. *Critical African Studies, 13*(1), 115–126.

Matulionyte, R., & Lee, J. (2022). Copyright in AI-generated works: Lessons from recent developments in patent law. *SCRIPTed: Journal of Law, Technology and Society, 19*(1), 5–35.

Mayer-Schönberger, V. (2005). In search of the story: Narratives of intellectual property. *Virginia Journal of Law & Technology, 10*(3), 1–19.

Merges, R. P. (2011). *Justifying intellectual property*. Harvard University Press.

Miernicki, M., & Ng, I. (2021). Artificial intelligence and moral rights. *AI & Society, 36*, 319–329.

Murray, M. D. (2023). Generative and AI authored artworks and copyright law. *Hastings Communications and Entertainment Law Journal, 45*(1), 27–44.

Naqvi, Z. (2020). Artificial intelligence, copyright, and copyright infringement. *Marquette Intellectual Property Law Review, 24*(1), 15–52.

Noto La Diega, G. (2023). *Internet of things and the law: Legal strategies for consumer-centric smart technologies*. Routledge.

Paquette, L. (2021). Artificial life imitating art imitating life: Copyright ownership in AI-generated works. *Intellectual Property Journal, 33*, 183–215.

Picht, P. G., & Thouvenin, F. (2023). AI and IP: Theory to policy and back again – Policy and research recommendations at the intersection of artificial intelligence and intellectual property. *IIC – International Review of Intellectual Property and Competition Law*, *54*, 916–940.

Pila, J., & Torremans, P. (2019). *European intellectual property law* (2nd ed.). Oxford University Press.

Posner, R. A. (2005). Intellectual property: The law and economics approach. *Journal of Economic Perspectives*, *19*(2), 57–73.

Ramalho, A. (2022). *Intellectual property protection for AI-generated creations: Europe, the United States, Australia and Japan.* Routledge.

Rosati, E. (2019). *Copyright and the Court of Justice of the European Union.* Oxford and New York: Oxford University Press.

Salami, E. (2021). AI-generated works and copyright law: Towards a union of strange bedfellows. *Journal of Intellectual Property Law & Practice*, *16*(2), 124–135.

Salzberger, E. M. (2011). The law and economics analysis of intellectual property: Paradigmatic Shift from incentives to traditional property. *Review of Law and Economics*, *7*(2), 435–480.

Senftleben, M., & Buijtelaar, L. (2020). *Robot creativity: An incentive-based neighboring rights approach* . https://papers.ssrn.com/sol3/papers. cfm?abstract_id=3707741.

Shtefan, A. (2021). Creativity and artificial intelligence: A view from the perspective of copyright. *Journal of Intellectual Property Law & Practice*, *16*(7), 720–728.

Spindler, G. (2022). AI and copyright law: The European perspective. In L. A. Di Matteo, C. Poncibò, & M. Cannarsa (Eds.), *The Cambridge handbook of artificial intelligence: Global perspectives on law and ethics* (pp. 257–269). Cambridge University Press.

Striphas, T., & McLeod, K. (2006). Strategic improprieties: Cultural studies, the everyday, and the politics of intellectual properties. *Cultural Studies*, *20*(2–3), 119–144.

Svedman, M. (2020). Artificial creativity: A case against copyright for AI-created visual artwork. *IP Theory*, *9*(4), 1–22.

Tehranian, J. (2012). Towards a critical IP theory: Copyright, consecration, and control. *Brigham Young University Law Review*, *4*, 1233–1290.

Wan, E., & Lu, H. (2021). Copyright protection for AI-generated outputs: The experience from China. *Computer Law & Security Review*, *42*, 1–11.

Wang, F. F. (2023). Copyright protection for AI-generated works: Solutions to further challenges from generative AI. *Amicus Curiae*, *5*(1), 88–103.

Yanisky-Ravid, S. (2017). Generating rembrandt: Artificial intelligence, copyright, and accountability in the 3A era: The human-like authors are already here: A new model. *Michigan State Law Review*, *4*, 659–726.

Yanisky-Ravid, S., & Velez-Hernandez, L. A. (2018). Copyrightability of artworks produced by creative Robots and originality: The formality-objective model. *Minnesota Journal of Law, Science & Technology*, *19*(1), 1–53.

Yılmaztekin, H. K. (2023). *Artificial intelligence, design law and fashion.* Routledge.

Zhi, T. (2021). Power-knowledge theory in intellectual property law. *Washington University Jurisprudence Review*, *14*(1), 279–306.

Zurth, P. (2021). A case against copyright protection for AI-generated works. *UCLA Journal of Law & Technology*, *25*(2), 1–18.

Treaties and Legislation

International

Agreement on Trade-Related Aspects of Intellectual Property Rights, Apr. 15, 1994, Marrakesh Agreement Establishing the World Trade Organization, Annex 1C, 1869 U.N.T.S. 299, 33 I.L.M. 1197 (1994).

Berne Convention for the Protection of Literary and Artistic Works (adopted 14 July 1967, entered into force 29 January 1970) 828 UNTS 221.

UN General Assembly, International Covenant on Economic, Social and Cultural Rights, 16 December 1966, United Nations, Treaty Series, vol. 993.

UN General Assembly, Universal Declaration of Human Rights, 10 December 1948, 217 A (III).

WIPO Copyright Treaty, Dec. 20, 1996, S. Treaty Doc. No. 105–17 (1997); 2186 U.N.T.S. 121; 36 I.L.M. 65 (1997).

European Union

Directive (EU) 2009/24/EC of the European Parliament and of The Council of 23 April 2009 on The Legal Protection of Computer Programs.

Directive (EU) 2019/790 of the European Parliament and of the Council of 17 April 2019 on Copyright and Related Rights in the Digital Single Market and Amending Directives 96/9/EC and 2001/29/EC.

Directive 96/9/EC of the European Parliament and of the Council of 11 March 1996 on the Legal Protection of Databases.

Japan

Copyright Act (Act No. 48 of May 6, 1970).

United States

Copyright, Designs and Patents Act 1988.
U.S. Copyright Act, 17 U.S.C.

United Kingdom

Copyright, Designs and Patents Act 1988.

Case Law

Court of Justice of the European Union

Cofemel – Sociedade de Vestuário SA v G-Star Raw CV (C-683/17) EU :C:20 19:721 (12 September 2019).

Eva-Maria Painer v Standard VerlagsGmbH and Others (C-145/10) EU:C:2011:798 (1 December 2011).
Fixtures Marketing Ltd v Organismos Prognostikon Agonon Podosfairou AE (OPAP) (C-444/02) EU:C:2004:697 (9 November 2004).
Football Dataco Ltd and Others v Yahoo! UK Ltd and Others (C-604/10) EU:C:2012:115 (1 March 2012).
Funke Medien NRW GmbH v Bundesrepublik Deutschland (C-469/17) EU:C:2019:623 (29 July 2019).
Infopaq International A/S v Danske Dagblades Forening (C-5/08) EU:C:2009:465 (16 July 2009).
Levola Hengelo BV v Smilde Foods BV (C-310/17) EU:C:2018:899 (13 November 2018).
SI and Brompton Bicycle Ltd v Chedech/Get2Get (C-833/18) EU:C:2020:461 (11 June 2020).
The British Horseracing Board Ltd and Others v William Hill Organization Ltd (C-203/02) EU:C:2004:695 (9 November 2004).

China

Beijing Film Law Firm v. Beijing Baidu Netcom Science & Technology Co., Ltd., Beijing Internet Court, (2018) Jing 0491 Min Chu No. 239.
Shenzhen Tencent Computer System Co Ltd v. Shanghai Yingxun Technology Co Ltd (2019). Guangdong 0305 Civil First Trial No 14010.

United States

Burrow-Giles Lithographic Company v. Sarony, 111 U.S. 53 (1884).
Community for Creative Non-Violence v. Reid, 490 U.S. 730 (1989).
Feist Publications, Inc. v. Rural Tel. Serv. Co., 499 U.S. 340 (1991).
Naruto v. Slater, No. 16–15469 (9th Cir. 2018).
Penguin Books v. New Christian Church, Full End., 262 F. Supp. 2d 251 (S.D.N.Y. 2003).
Urantia Foundation v. Maaherra, 114 F.3d 955, 958 (9th Cir. 1997).

Other

U.S. Copyright Office. *Compendium of copyright office practices* (3rd ed.). www.copyright.gov/comp3/docs/compendium.pdf.

4 Subsidising Humans – Can It Work?

The precarity of conditions under which many artists and those employed in the creative industries live calls for strategies to ensure at least their basic quality of life. In some cases, this can even happen beyond 'traditional' income. Alacovska (2022, p. 674), for example, explores how artists engage in 'wageless life' practices by relying on 'barter, favour-swapping and commoning', in addition to 'alternative modes of consumption such as self-provisioning, sharing, thrift, repairing and downshifting', to explain how creators 'endure in the profession in spite of rampant precarity in the creative industries'. Indeed, it is no stretch to identify precarity as 'a fundamental element of creative work, characterized by high levels of insecure, unprotected and unremunerated work' (Alacovska, 2022, p. 675). Although sometimes a wageless life can be idealised as a harbinger of an alternative, post-capitalist, economy, one should also not ignore the tensions, threats, and constraints of such a life: after all, through the use of these alternative strategies, precarity is only mitigated rather than overcome (Alacovska, 2022, p. 688). Hence, it is argued here that economic incentives remain crucial in overcoming precarity. Moreover, as shown in the preceding chapters, since the emergence of generative AI has the potential to significantly increase such precarity, additional means for protecting the livelihoods of human creators should be sought. In addition, AI is likely to transform the structure of incentives that keep humans occupied in creative endeavours, as it essentially undercuts human authors and raises the prospect of a slowdown in creativity due to a resulting drop in human artistic creation (De Cremer et al., 2023). The effects of the explosion of AI-generated content are also likely to be exacerbated by some of the already-existing market conditions due to ever-growing amounts of available content and shrinking audience attentions spans, with AI adding a new dimension of 'unlimited content on demand' (De Cremer et al., 2023). Accordingly, remunerating or subsidising human authors becomes a topical issue.

DOI: 10.4324/9781003464976-4

4.1   The Opportunities and Challenges of Licencing

As already argued in this book, although the effects of generative AI may be felt less strongly in the fine arts segment and the top stratum of the artistic pecking order, human authors who have not achieved star status and those working in the creative industries are likely to have their incomes significantly affected, creating the need for compensation or even retraining schemes (Senftleben, 2023). However, this does not discard the possibility of still remunerating and incentivising human authors. In fact, one could argue that the provision of compensation or remuneration not only serves the traditional functions that have long been used to justify copyright – namely, societal and cultural progress – but is arguably in the interest of the AI industry itself since the development of new human art styles and movements results in new training data and, therefore, more diverse AI-generated content (Senftleben, 2023).

One option might be to attempt a return to business as usual by simply driving a wedge between human authors and AI content generation, thereby trying to preserve the traditional modes of remuneration and incentivisation. There are increasing possibilities for human authors to opt out of their works being used for the training of generative AI models (see, e.g., Heikkilä, 2022; Wiggers, 2022). However, simply opting out cannot protect an author from competition with AI as there will still likely be sufficient data in the training set for the model to generate new content. In fact, given the size of training datasets, opt-outs are expected to have only very limited effect on the end model. As Kelly (2022) notes, if the artist opting out is not an influential one, then the results generated from the dataset will be the same since their works would not have had a notable effect; meanwhile, if they *are* influential, then they would have impacted the works of other artists who, potentially, may not have opted out. Moreover, the opt-out mechanism unfairly puts the onus on authors as they become the ones responsible for keeping their works from being used and thus not only have to be informed about the need to opt out but also have to take positive action. Still, even if an author opts out, they cannot be sure that their work would not have been used, as training data are normally not made public. Moreover, although Article 4 of the Digital Single Market (DSM) Directive provides for an opt out mechanism, 'generally recognized standards or protocols for the machine-readable expression of the reservation' are currently lacking (Keller & Warso, 2023). Another solution could be to exclude living artists from AI training databases altogether to avoid generative models mimicking their style (see, e.g., Nolan, 2022). Nevertheless, this would limit only one strand of competition (direct imitation). Furthermore, alternative, more progressivist views are also presented. For example, Kelly (2022) predicts a future in which artists are 'fighting one another to be included in the training set' because '[i]f an artist is in the main pool, their influence will be shared and felt by all', while others would be condemned to obscurity. This, however, would effectively mean artists fighting to be exploited unless inclusion also brings some material benefits and incentives.

Instead, licencing and collective rights management options could be seen as simpler solutions that, instead of – potentially futile – opt-out mechanisms, would allow authors to benefit from AI-generated content. It would indeed make sense to reward human authors at the AI training stage as this is the occasion when their works are being used (Senftleben, 2023). However, since such remuneration would have to deal with large and fragmented pools of authors, collective societies would need to act as intermediaries. Crucially, remunerating authors through collective societies could potentially solve several thorny issues: first, this would allow human authors to supplement their income and earn from their works being used for AI training purposes, while for AI companies, this would provide easier access to the necessary training data without the need to approach individual authors in what would be an extremely time-consuming process (Selvadurai & Matulionyte, 2020, p. 542). Such collective management organisations, acting as administrators of licences that track (and, in some cases, facilitating) the use of copyrighted works while also collecting and distributing payments for such use, could add significant efficiencies (Priest, 2021, pp. 5–6).

Škiljić (2021, p. 1355) proposes the establishment of collective licencing schemes with compulsory licencing and sees this as a way to combine the rapid development of the generative AI industry with the need to remunerate creators (see also Senftleben, 2023). Collective licencing is of particular importance here because it reduces transaction costs in reaching agreements between creators and users or their works and in distributing income through collective rights management; the latter is also beneficial to the authors in terms of making administration and enforcement more efficient and cheaper (Priest, 2021, p. 2; see also Gervais, 2019). The danger, however, is that should collective management organisations become gateway monopolists to accessing artistic content, they may end up charging unfairly high prices for access (Priest, 2021, p. 2). However, in the context of online content abundance, Gervais (2019, p. 504) argues that protected works need to compete with freely available content, and if their use is expensive or cumbersome, monetisation options would dwindle; in this context, collective rights management organisations would, as part of their function, maintain both ease of access and competitive pricing. The overarching logic here would be that even minuscule income would be better than none.

Collective, perhaps even statutory, licencing could help solve one of the outstanding issues that otherwise complicates remuneration efforts: that of the inconvenience of one-on-one contracts between content creators and AI companies, thereby not hindering innovation in the field but simultaneously enabling authors to be remunerated for the use of their works for commercial AI training purposes (Geiger & Iaia, 2024, p. 6; Geiger et al., 2024). Here, notably, although simple collective licencing is voluntary and is therefore sub-optimal from a user perspective, by leaving part of the works more difficult to obtain for use, whether compulsory or statutory, licencing removes the need for obtaining permissions while still retaining author remuneration (Priest, 2021, pp. 4–5). As argued by Geiger and Iaia (2024, p. 7), statutory licencing is essential for progress in both the technological and artistic domains because otherwise, 'the productive capacity of Generative AI-based tools – and their power to assist human beings reaching new artistic and scientific results – risks being left partially unrealized' (see also Geiger et al., 2024). Meanwhile, reliance on a limited sample of works that are in the public domain, which can lawfully be acquired using text and data mining techniques, or that have been created by authors subscribing to voluntary licencing schemes, 'marginalizes the heterogeneity of AI-generated outputs, thus increasing their homologation rate and the likelihood of biases' (Geiger & Iaia, 2024, p. 7). Statutory licenc-ing is thereby seen as simultaneously maximising *both* the amount of train-ing material available for machine learning and the remuneration for authors (Geiger & Iaia, 2024, p. 7). In the EU, for example, particularly since the adoption of the Directive on Copyright in the DSM Directive (see, especially, Articles 8–12), there has been a move towards substituting the traditional opt-in principle of licencing with opt-out clauses and, following Article 17 of the same Directive, facilitating the licencing of content to sharing and streaming platforms (for a discussion, see, e.g., de la Durantaye, 2022). In this way, some claim, the otherwise conflicting demands of the increased availability of material for future creativity and the remuneration of current authors can be reconciled (Geiger et al., 2024). It is feasible to apply a similar model vis-à-vis machine learning for generative AI purposes.

Still, this might not be without complications. Although it might be intui-tive to remunerate authors on the basis of their work having been used to train AI models, which is in a way, not dissimilar to remuneration for the public use of authors' works, in this case, such a mechanism would be unfeasible. This is because due to AI models having been trained on extremely large data-sets that encompass cultural knowledge as a whole, in many cases, it would be very difficult, if at all possible, to demonstrate that a specific work has been consequential in the generation of a given output; moreover, even if such demonstration was possible, the size of the sample from which a specific generation process had been drawn would likely be so large that the adminis-tration of such a collection would no longer be feasible while any returns to the authors would only be marginal. In essence, it must be kept in mind that '[i]f it is difficult to isolate the contribution made by any single input, this is because no input contributes in isolation' (Drott, 2021, p. 202). Similarly, as Merkley (2023) asserts,

Individual human endeavour does not have an individual value once it is dissolved into the algorithm; the value is, at best, collective and would be, in the database of 5 billion works, miniscule and impossible to assign to any one human.

Gervais (2019, p. 498) also shares a similar opinion (albeit without discarding the possibility of collective licencing) by emphasising how value in collective licencing is located not in individual works (whose input becomes almost impossible to evaluate independently) but in the aggregate offering, that is, the total repertoire being licenced, but as the repertoire grows, the share received by each individual creator shrinks. This is even more pressing given the omnivorous nature of AI.

Kelly (2022), for example, goes even further and argues against remuneration in principle by underscoring that all artists have been influenced by others, both while developing their style and as already established artists, but there is no expectation of such influences being paid for – contrary to the attitudes towards generative AI. Nevertheless, one could counter-argue that in the case of machine learning, the use of existing works goes beyond mere influence – they are the *substance* of AI-generated content, not a mere side influence. Likewise, in generative AI, such influence goes beyond mere individual-level creative encounters and enters the domain of for-profit mass production. A more substantive argument, however, is that, admittedly, the boundaries of influence are porous, which makes attributions of any specific work's influence (and, therefore, the distribution of remuneration) arbitrary (Kelly, 2022). Meanwhile, Dermawan (2023) argues for a broad text and data mining (TDM) exception based on the Japanese copyright law principle of non-enjoyment: because, as the argument goes, it is the enjoyment derived from accessing and consuming a work that constitutes the work's remunerable value, all uses that are not motivated by direct enjoyment should be permitted; given that content scraping tools and machine learning systems are neither capable of nor driven by the aesthetic and other forms of enjoyment when accessing works, any such automated use should be freely permitted. An alternative provision of incentives to artists would therefore be necessary if this approach is accepted. To this effect, a universal subsidy as described subsequently in this chapter, although not without its own drawbacks, would allow for remuneration in a way that is simple and transparent.

Moreover, the rising prominence of synthetic data (i.e., data not collected from the environment but generated by AI tools) for training machine learning models in fields where 'genuine' data are unavailable, too expensive, overly sensitive, etc. (see, e.g., Jacobsen, 2023) means that, particularly should the copyright infringement cases currently before courts succeed, generative AI companies could move beyond using human authors' works for training purposes. As a result, attempts at establishing systems for licencing or collective rights management would also be adversely impacted. Moreover, licencing schemes would have the effect of favouring the already large and wealthy companies that could pay authors for using their works and would thus further entrench the dominance of the incumbents, while newcomers would likely be barred from entry into the market due to prohibitive upfront costs (Selvadurai & Matulionyte, 2020, p. 541). Nevertheless, as the same authors admit, the opposite does not offer a favourable outcome either: if large companies can develop their models in an unrestricted way by reaping the benefits and failing to share them with human artists (who are effectively rendered free data labourers), the market dominance of such companies (and, even more so, the gap between the individual and the corporate production of creative outcomes) would only increase (Selvadurai & Matulionyte, 2020, p. 541). Hence, there does not seem to be an easy way out of this conundrum, at least should one remain within the licencing framework.

Arguably, a possible solution to the complexities of remuneration at the input stage would be to flip the entire scheme and to provide remuneration at the output stage. Here, a levy could be imposed on AI tools or on the output produced by them and the income redistributed to authors, likely in combination with mandatory licencing (Senftleben, 2023). As an additional benefit, Senftleben (2023, p. 1537) explains that this might make AI-generated content more expensive, thereby reducing the disadvantage suffered by human authors and at least somewhat levelling the playing field. In this way, the taxation of generative AI companies and sectoral redistribution through, for example, a narrowed-down version of Universal Basic Income (UBI) (e.g., in the form of an author's stipend) might be an appealing solution. Should this be financed through, for example, a tax on revenue or profits, this would also imply a proportionate distribution of the burden among emergent startups and already well-established companies. Nevertheless, some (see, e.g., Naqvi, 2020) argue that any taxation of AI use would end up being counterproductive as it would harm industry development. An alternative system of taxation could focus not on developers who already face high costs of developing new AI models but on specific uses of AI tools (for example, a tax on the users of such tools), which is not dissimilar to, for example, ecology-focused taxes on vehicles (Naqvi, 2020). A argument could be made that such income would not be a mere subsidy or some other form of altruistic handout but a 'rightful share': since the wealth generated by technologies depends on the data that have been socially generated by individuals (e. g., authors, artists, etc.), these individuals must receive a dividend on what they have produced (Fouksman & Klein, 2019, p. 496–498), and it is the end beneficiaries (i.e., the end users) who would have to pay. Still, this system would be less transparent (by introducing an extra step or an intermediary between the payer and the beneficiary) and would likely foster a market for the illegal use of generative outputs, which is not dissimilar from the current problem of audiovisual content piracy.

4.2   Changing Societal Paradigms: Towards a Post-Work Future?

In light of the impending possibility (and in some cases, already reality) of automation, an entire body of literature has sprung up that could be broadly described as post-work. By taking such increasing automation as a given, authors involved in this strand of thinking tend to adopt a generally positive stance on the future in which work is scarce or has been eliminated altogether. Technological change, it is often claimed, will have unprecedented long-term effects, since not only physical, menial, or low- and medium-skill tasks but also intellectual, creative, and high-skill tasks could end up being automated and replaced (de Sio et al., 2021, p. 3). It is crucial to underline that the argument of technological change is often deterministic and linear: social and political agency, context and sector variation, and other factors are conveniently omitted, and the focus instead is on a progressivist outlook whereby if something can happen, it simply will, allegedly bringing about a major paradigm shift (Howcroft & Taylor, 2023, p. 352). Similarly, de Sio et al. (2021, p. 5) underscore how technological unemployment is often perceived to be 'destiny'. Instead, particularly if left uncontested, technological change typically happens with the interests of those in power taking centre stage (Howcroft & Taylor, 2023). For this reason, even when discussing the possibility of a post-work future, a focus on who are the end beneficiaries, how they would benefit, and on the interests driving this potential future has to be maintained.

In considerations of a post-work future, two aspects are typically taken into account. The first and most discussed is economic, whereby as a result of automation, 'it is reasonable to consider a long-term future where having a paid job is no longer the key determinant for one's access to resources' and 'to being able to make a living' (Hines, 2019, p. 20). The second and more overlooked aspect is the social and psychological dimension that underpins substitution, whereby the positive values, such as identity, self-esteem, and interpersonal interactions, are seen to be easily replicable also in out-of-work contexts (see, e.g., Tegmark, 2017, p. 129). In either case, however, the debate on the technological substitution of jobs is connected to the utopia of a society of abundance in which work is no longer necessary for individuals to live affluent lives, with technology becoming a straight path towards human flourishing (Spencer, 2023, p. 1). There is even an emancipatory drive that focuses on the need to 'liberate humanity from the drudgery of work' (Srnicek & Williams, 2015, p. 109) and 'dynamics of exploitation' (Allegri & Foschi, 2021, p. 15). Automation is thus also perceived as generating 'an abundance of wealth' (Hines, 2019, p. 20). The expectation is that of guaranteed 'well-being for all, funded by part of the wealth that future AI generates', thereby enabling society to 'flourish like never before': it is alleged that 'once one breaks free of the constraint that everyone's activities must generate income, the sky's the limit' (Tegmark, 2017, p. 129), with individuals being able to fulfil their aspirations without the need to worry about income – that is, they have the freedom to pursue their own self-development, engage in creative endeavours, etc. (Allegri & Foschi, 2021, p. 15). Consequently, should one follow such optimistic accounts, instead of being feared, automation and job loss should be encouraged.

Some scholars are more sceptical and emphasise that levels at which a truly universal basic income or other form of direct or indirect handouts would still be affordable to states are likely to allow individuals only to subsist but not to invest in self-development, skill acquisition, or other costly pursuits (see, e.g., de Sio et al., 2021). Nevertheless, the general mood in this line of thinking tends to be positive, especially as such a post-work future is said to usher in a life of happiness, community involvement, and transcendental pursuits, specifically, one in which humans will once again have time to engage in noble activities (Etzioni, 2017), with a notable caveat that this would be a world of slavery – just of robot slaves this time. Even leaving the ethical implications of such a view aside, notably, the implementation of such arrangements would necessitate complete societal transformation. For other academics, the focus is more on being able to dedicate oneself to caring for others and other noble pursuits (Perkins et al., 2022). Notably, post-work societies are not necessarily imagined as societies of idleness – it is also argued that once labour becomes untied from the need to earn a living, it can become a means to 'express our species being' (Avis, 2020, p. 85). This point of view could tie in well with engagement in artistic pursuits and other beneficial outcomes. Attempts at achieving automated leisure are already evident in, for example, 'life hacking' communities that aim to use the latest software and tools to maximise their productivity and income while minimising actual work (see, notably, Reagle, 2019). Particularly, as can be judged from this discussion, even among the optimists, there tends to be a tension as to the ultimate moral impetus of transitioning towards a post-work society: between an individualistic gain-focused and a more community-focused altruistic future.

Particularly regarding the artistic domain but potentially, also beyond, generative AI companies are seen as those that could be at the source of societal wealth. They are particularly perceived as needing to compensate society (or at least, human artists) for their own success. The argument goes that as generative AI companies appropriate the outcome of human creativity as such, they withdraw some of the value inherent in this output – value that would otherwise allow this specific stratum of human society to reproduce itself (Drott, 2021, p. 202). A more pressing concern would therefore be an equitable distribution of the gains of technological innovation – namely, making sure that the benefits are not concentrated in the hands of a few large actors (Hertzmann, 2018, p. 14; see also Peukert, 2019, pp. 204–206). This latter point is particularly pressing: while it might be soothing to expect that AI will become a mere tool in the artists' hands that removes the boring and repetitive aspects of work and provides a new means of inspiration and expression (see, e.g., Hertzmann, 2018, p. 15), in actual practice, the creative deployment of AI is likely to become primarily a corporate playground. Peukert (2019, p. 199) hints at one corroborating factor (albeit without explicitly making such a connection) by identifying how online platforms have become capable of dissecting audience needs and interests and tailoring content accordingly so that users are almost bound to like what is being offered to them. Surely, it would hardly be possible for human artists to engage in such an ambitious tailoring of their works, which means that without such platforms, the amount of audience attention likely to be attracted would increasingly dwindle. The capture of economic rents by taxing AI (either the development or use of such technology) would be essential to providing the means of subsistence in a post-work (or limited-work) society (Perkins et al., 2022). Indeed, an argument can be made that if it is the mining and monetisation of data (including works of art as data) that are at the heart of economic growth and the driver of the profits earned by technology companies, then those who generate such data should be justly remunerated (Lamchek, 2020; see also Allegri & Foschi, 2021). Another possible source of argument could be derived from the right to benefit from scientific progress, which is enshrined in Article 27 of the UDHR and Article 15 of the ICESCR, including a potential entitlement to UBI if it is funded by the economic benefits of scientific innovation, such as advancements in AI (Lamchek, 2020). This, however, if put in practice, would have to be balanced in a way to not to stifle progress and to not limit the ability of start-ups and new actors to enter the market.

Nevertheless, there does seem to be an element of stick and carrot in at least some discussions of post-work: on the one hand, promises of wealth, while on the other hand, visions of definite societal restructuring. Accordingly, there are expectations that the job displacement caused by automation is more significant than that resulting from previous technological disruptions, which undermines the capacity of compensating job losses through entrepreneurship-inspired growth (D'Mello, 2019). The idea has typically been that although technological innovations unavoidably create disruptions in the job market by destroying some jobs or obliterating entire professions, entrepreneurs that drive new economic ventures (including entrepreneurship as it is understood in the cultural industries) would create just as many or even more economic opportunities. This, however, is often seen as no longer being the case in light of advances in AI.

Considering this, some intellectuals resort to technological determinism by citing the unavoidable 'sociocultural effects of artificial creativity' (Dornis, 2020, p. 40) and relating them to the wider predictions of a post-work society. Since changes in the labour market, according to this view, are unavoidable, it is only natural that artists share the fate of their fellow humans who are going to lose their jobs due to automation. In this way, the allegedly unavoidable substitution of human-made artworks with AI-generated ones 'not only increases the consumption of creative products and makes them cheaper, but also frees up human resources for use in higher-quality employment, more social and empathetic commitments, and the enjoyment of leisure time' (Dornis, 2020, p. 42). Hence, for Lim (2018, p. 827), '[i]t is futile for Luddites to fight over obsolete technologies and yesterday's jobs' – including those in creative endeavours. Following the proponents of this scenario, just like the representatives of other professions, '[s]ome outclassed human creators will find their livelihoods challenged if they are unable or unwilling to retrain, retool, and use AI to augment their work to remain relevant' (Lim, 2018, p. 854; for a similar argument, see, e.g., Hertzmann 2018, pp. 14–15). Although those representing the view of artistic creativity as a utilitarian exchange might find the general spirit of such assertions agreeable, from the moral rights standpoint, in the equation of creative artistic practices with, for example, the drudgery of the factory floor, both activities being posited as having an identical need to be liberated does seem to be an overstretch.

Crucially, if work is no longer seen as necessary (or, indeed, available) and full employment can no longer serve as a prosperity-generating policy in a future society, then new forms of income have to be considered (Spencer, 2023, pp. 3–4). In general, visions of a post-work future tend to posit some versions of UBI as perhaps the only or at least the main antidote to a potential future in which poverty and a lack of meaning would otherwise abound (see, e.g., Simms, 2019, p. 46). Regarding human authors, UBI might be seen as a return to an earlier state of affairs prior to the emergence of early forms of copyright in the eighteenth century: namely, authors rely not on market sales of their goods but on patronage (Potts, 2023, p. 9). For example, Potts (2023, p. 129) argues that a verbatim return to this system might be a realistic option, but this would do little to eradicate or weaken the precarity faced by authors, and their livelihood would then depend on securing and retaining the support of their patrons. Meanwhile, a guaranteed Author's Income could potentially enable engagement in (somewhat) unhindered creativity.

As Drott (2021) observes, the companies behind generative AI models effectively free ride on the labour of human authors not only in terms of specific works that are mined but also in the broader sense of gauging genre and stylistic conventions. However, they can also be seen to go further: they not only feed on human authors' labour but also undermine these authors by taking away commercial opportunities. Therefore, the harm suffered as AI learns to imitate human creative endeavours truly manifests itself not only at the individual level but also at the aggregate level, negatively impacting the market as a whole (Drott, 2021, p. 202) and thus necessitating collective remedies. One such collective solution could be the implementation of some version of UBI.

Certainly, UBI, or a variant thereof, is not the only option. For example, technologically enabled forms of contemporary patronage, either ad hoc (such as crowdfunding campaigns) or post hoc (such as various platforms offering subscription-based access to content), could be seen as potential solutions.

Nevertheless, given that it is actually rare for crowdfunding campaigns to reach the required threshold and that the majority of artists offering their works on a subscription basis struggle to earn a living and have to also rely on additional income, the potential of such alternatives does seem limited or perhaps supplementary (Potts, 2023, pp. 130–131). Thus, a more predictable and organised form of income for authors seems to be necessary if sufficient incentivisation to keep them in artistic endeavours is to be maintained.

4.3   The Possibility of Author's Basic Income

Given the advances in artificial creativity, it should perhaps come as little surprise that some would simply declare the struggle for artist incentivisation to have already been lost and instead propose UBI as a solution (see, e.g., Naqvi, 2020, p. 28). Indeed, currently, perhaps the most important driving factor behind the appeal of UBI is technological innovation, particularly concerning the fears of technological unemployment as humans are replaced by AI (Straubhaar, 2017, p. 75). Typically, UBI is defined as 'an income paid by a political community to all its members on an individual basis, without [a] means test or work requirement' (Van Parijs, 2004, p. 8). In this sense, the 'universal' part of UBI certainly lives up to its promise (Straubhaar, 2017, p. 74; Furman & Seamans, 2019). In more technology-focused versions, UBI simply becomes a means to ameliorate actual or potential job loss in light of automation rather than some ambitious project for social reform (see, e.g., Haglin et al., 2023). In standard depictions, UBI is seen to possess three characteristics: it is available to all (hence, universal), it provides monetary benefits (instead of various forms of in-kind support), and it is unconditional (which further strengthens the universality aspect) (see, e.g., Furman & Seamans, 2019, p. 180; Harris, 2023, pp. 2–3). Essentially, UBI could thus be interpreted 'as a social dividend of the digital era' that allows individuals to make use of the wealth that is collectively produced anyway (through datafication, a platform economy, etc.) but that otherwise remains confined among the big technology companies (Allegri & Foschi 2021, p. 17).

In a sense, UBI might seem counter-intuitive from the common standpoint of contemporary societies: while 'essentially all modern welfare states are productivist, in the sense that they are concerned with ensuring the smooth supply of labour to productive sectors of the economy', and assuming work as the 'normal' condition for all able individuals, the innovation of UBI is 'a decoupling of income entitlements from income-earning activities' (Kozák, 2021, p. 25). However, others see UBI and productivity as complementary. In fact, UBI is even claimed to contribute to economic pursuits: as entrepreneurship can be considered as necessitating at least some degree of privilege (being able to afford taking risks and engaging in activities that, although potentially rewarding in the future, may not initially produce income or be even costly), having guaranteed income might ease such a burden, thereby increasing economic opportunities for all (D'Mello, 2019, p. 309; see also Perkins et al., 2022). For now, the core ethical concerns about AI are 'driven by a fundamental concern for human emancipation and empowerment' (Waelen, 2022, p. 11) whereby human choices are determined by their aptitudes and desires rather than monetary considerations.

When considering the feasibility of applying the UBI model to authors to compensate for their livelihoods being adversely affected by AI, two pathways are available. The first would mean waiting for a blanket implementation of full UBI across all sectors of society. However, in this case, the measure would lose its exclusivity both as a compensation for authors for the loss of efficiency of copyright protection and, therefore, as an incentivising factor for the creation of new works. The second option would be to reject the universality of UBI and apply the payment on a sectoral basis – that is, the creation of Author's Basic Income (ABI) – to compensate for the lost or decreased financial incentives in light of the growing prominence of generative AI. In this way, ABI would acquire a redistributive function: most likely by taxing the digital wealth generated from the data produced by individuals (in this particular case, authors) to effectively remunerate them for their otherwise unpaid labour (see generally Fouksman & Klein, 2019). Such a 'Robin Hood' nature of generalist UBI has already been demonstrated to increase its appeal among citizens, thereby making political adoption easier (Rincón et al., 2022). This, however, would move beyond the 'post-work' framework with which UBI and similar proposals have become commonly associated: labour (in this case, creative labour) would be seen here as persistent, albeit in an immaterial – digital – form. This solution is not completely new: for example, with the rise of digital content (and it therefore becoming cheaply and easily copiable), charges and levies on storage, starting with audio cassettes to the current means of content storage, have been used to compensate those adversely impacted by the eroding market for their work, with the Audio Home Recording Act in the US being the first major piece of legislation to this effect (see, e.g., Sobel, 2017, p. 91), although it was more directly focused to benefit corporate actors in the creative industries.

In addition to being a (seemingly) simple solution, UBI (or some narrower version thereof, including one targeted specifically at human authors), sits rather comfortably with the human rights obligations of states. As part of the economic and social rights framework, the right to social security (UDHR Art. 22; ICESCR Art. 9) puts an onus on states to provide at least a minimal and progressively increasing level of economic protection and basic services to their citizens (see, e.g., Engström, 2019) so that people can enjoy an adequate standard of living (UDHR Art. 25). In effect, a basic standard of living has to be ensured even in the face of the other needs and/or severe economic constraints that a state might be facing (UN Committee on Economic, Social and Cultural Rights (CESCR), General Comment 19). Likewise, Article 11 of the ICESCR provides for a right to an adequate standard of living, which is of no lesser relevance in this context. In addition, there is a direct link between social security, provided in cash or in kind, and the Sustainable Development Goals (Engström, 2019). Certainly, there is nothing to suggest that UBI – or for that matter, ABI – could be a *necessary* or the *only* measure to ensure the adequate standard of human well-being, particularly if similar results could be achieved by more traditional welfare measures (Goldblatt, 2020, p. 82).

A more nuanced case to this effect is provided by the right to work and just remuneration principles, including the ability to freely choose and accept one's work (UDHR Art. 23; ICESCR Art. 6). It is clear that UBI, in whatever form, would likely strengthen the ability to choose work and be selective about what individuals accept to do because paid work would be decoupled from subsistence (Goldblatt, 2020, p. 82; Kabasakal Arat & Waring, 2022, p. 61). Likewise, individuals would be empowered to choose work that might not necessarily provide an adequate standard of living on its own, such as creative work. Moreover, since 'full and productive employment' remains a goal to be progressively realised (typical of economic, social, and cultural rights) rather than a right that can be resorted to here and now (CESCR, General Comment 18, Art. 41), measures to bridge the gap between the absence of full employment and the necessity to maintain an adequate standard of living have to be put in place. However, it must also be emphasised that existing human rights standards have been developed in a framework that is still premised upon 'a contingent relation between employment and subsistence, mediated by the wage' (Kabasakal Arat & Waring, 2022, p. 62). Arguably, technological developments, particularly in terms of automation, have disrupted such widely assumed premises, paradoxically re-rendering human rights (particularly the right to work) as a conservative force that redirects attention from the introduction of potential new solutions, such as UBI (Kabasakal Arat & Waring, 2022). Moreover, interpretation also matters: for example, traditionally, the right to work and social security has been interpreted in a collectivist way, as a collective entitlement to benefit from growth, whereas a more individualised view focused on the capacity for individual flourishing and self-realisation has come to prevail (see, e.g., Leisering, 2020). Ultimately, Article 28 of the UDHR postulates an entitlement 'to a social and international order in which the rights and freedoms set forth in this Declaration can be fully realized', thereby putting an onus on states to consider human rights holistically and come up with ways to ensure successful implementation and underscoring the inseparability among economic, social, and cultural rights on the one hand and civic and political rights on the other hand (Marks, 2022).

Automation can be seen as narrowing 'the domain for genuinely meaningful action', whereby 'we could build a world of abundance in which machines solve most moral problems . . ., make new and interesting discoveries in which we can delight, and in which we are richly rewarded by their technological acceleration', but simultaneously, such advancement would be of a lesser value to humans because 'we will be the passive recipients of these benefits, not active contributors to them' (Danaher, 2017, p. 72). Individuals thus end up losing their autonomy as they increasingly live in environments pre-structured by algorithms and automated modes of governance (Danaher, 2019). UBI or a sectoral version thereof might be seen as both legitimising and incentivising such passivity and the mere recipiency of a technologized society's outcomes. At the same time, however, an argument can also be made concerning the dangers of missing out on opportunities, including those of greater efficiency and rationality (and otherwise superior decision-making) and behavioural correction supposedly ushered in by ever more pervasive algorithmic governance and broad-scale automation: in effect, then, any limitations of autonomy may be compensated for by 'simply replacing or off-setting other autonomy-undermining practices' (Danaher, 2019, p. 110). UBI thus does raise important questions about societal duties (such as meaningful contributions by individuals to their societies, through work or otherwise) and rights (such as the right to social protection) by amplifying rights and reducing duties (Dumont, 2022, p. 308). Similarly, Kozák (2021, p. 24) underscores 'the contrast between the non-productivist nature of [UBI's] underlying principles and the productivist normative foundations of modern societies'. In this sense, guaranteed income based on contributions in a particular sector (art in the case of ABI) might help de-radicalise the proposition.

As might be expected, a crucial point of contention even among adherents of UBI remains the size of such payments: some expect it to be sufficient for survival (or even for a comfortable lifestyle), thereby eliminating the need for work altogether (hence, being fully 'post-work'), while others frame it more as a top-up, an additional source of income that would ease economic tensions and reduce precarity but that still requires productive involvement in the economy (see, e.g., Harris, 2023, p. 3). Indeed, economic unsustainability is perhaps the main criticism of UBI – as providing a universal regular payment to all citizens of a state could be prohibitively expensive (Allegri & Foschi, 2021, p. 13). Although suggestions for financing UBI range from a 'robot tax' to high levels of taxation on any remaining sources of income (interest, some vestiges of labour-related income, etc.) and corporate profits, the main positive trade-off is seen in terms of providing not merely a safety net but also a measure of a comfortable life open for experimentation and creativity (Straubhaar, 2017; see also Allegri & Foschi, 2021, p. 17). The premise, however, is that creativity is a universal attribute whose realisation is not dependent on incentives but merely on the presence of sufficient free time. This, however, is only the first of the challenges that arise when considering the feasibility of ABI (as a limited in scope UBI) as a replacement for the loss of incentives for the creation of artistic works.

Notably, especially for the more simplistic accounts of UBI, the criticism is that it is supposed to work as a magic silver bullet that solves all problems at once without first considering the root causes of the underlying issues, which may have more to do with the underlying forms of social, economic, and political organisation (Manza, 2023). Hence, a common charge against UBI is that if it is simply introduced on top of the existing distribution of wealth, then it would do nothing to reduce the inequalities already present in society: as Avis (2020, p. 84) frames the problem, 'its effectiveness as a counter to poverty would be undermined by its universality which would mirror existing patterns of inequality'. What an introduction of UBI *would* do, under this line of argument, is mainly justify existing power and material hierarchies by making them more palatable and *superficially* inclusive or even worse, buy support for some of the exploitative practices resulting from automation and tech sector-led growth (see Kelly, 2022; for more of the power asymmetries in shaping technological development, see Howcroft & Taylor, 2023). Similarly, for Fouksman and Klein (2019), both power and income asymmetries would be retained but made less visible, thereby precluding opportunities for truly radical change. Moreover, such inequality would be retained not only on a national but also on an international level where only rich and developed countries would be able to afford meaningful levels of UBI (Manza, 2023) or ABI.

There is also a potential criticism of UBI: instead of simplifying government payouts, UBI would only increase them and simultaneously extend the pervasiveness of authorities' control. As Dumont (2022, p. 302) argues, necessities for a functioning UBI include 'an exhaustive and up-to-date register of the entire eligible population, a reliable payment system that would effectively reach all those entitled to it . . . and a control system to monitor the system and rectify any errors', as well as an administrative apparatus to oversee it all. Specifically, regarding ABI, the obstacles are likely to be even more significant. In particular, the question of who counts as an author and is therefore entitled to such a subsidy looms large. In the case of authors' income, the tension between duties and rights would also likely result in a difficult, if at all possible, balance between productivity and idleness. On the one hand, if eligibility is assessed on the basis of continuously 'being an author', then this would create pressure to retain a qualifying standard (e.g., fulfil a creative work production quota) at all costs, potentially beyond the point of societal benefit (e.g., by sacrificing quality, thereby undermining the very purpose of incentivising creativity). On the other hand, making such income a lifelong entitlement would also undermine the purpose of incentivising (continued) creativity as authors would lack motivation to produce new creative works once having qualified for ABI. Although raising the threshold to qualify for permanent eligibility so that only 'deserving' creators are rewarded with lifelong income might seem like a potential solution, in practice, this would do nothing to ameliorate the precarious condition of the majority of human creators and would particularly harm young, up-and-coming creators struggling to qualify for the coveted status. A further complication is also one pertaining to the difficulties typically associated with determining artistry and creativity and the unavoidable debates as to the social and economic 'value' of a particular author's works that would ensue as a result. Consequently, the feasibility of ABI is very doubtful and once again leaves the question of author incentivisation open.

Bibliography

Alacovska, A. (2022). The wageless life of creative workers: Alternative economic practices, commoning and consumption work in cultural labour. *Sociology, 56*(4), 673–692.

Allegri, G., & Foschi, R. (2021). Universal basic income as a promoter of real freedom in a digital future. *World Futures, 77*(1), 1–22.

Avis, J. (2020). *Vocational education in the fourth industrial revolution: Education and employment in a post-work age.* Palgrave Macmillan.

D'Mello, J. F. (2019). Universal basic income and entrepreneurial pursuit in an autonomous society. *Journal of Management Inquiry, 28*(3), 306–310.

Danaher, J. (2017). Building a post-work utopia: Technological unemployment, life extension and the future of human flourishing. In K. LaGrandeur & J. J. Huges (Eds.), *Surviving the machine age: Intelligent technology and the transformation of human work* (pp. 63–82). Palgrave Macmillan.

Danaher, J. (2019). The ethics of algorithmic outsourcing in everyday life. In K. Yeung & M. Lodge (Eds.), *Algorithmic Regulation* (pp. 98–118). Oxford University Press.

De Cremer, D., Bianzino, N. M., & Falk, B. (2023, April 13). How generative AI could disrupt creative work. *Harvard Business Review.* https://hbr.org/2023/04/how-generative-ai-could-disrupt-creative-work.

de la Durantaye, K. (2022). Back to basics – European copyright law after the DSM directive. *IIC – International Review of Intellectual Property and Competition Law, 53*, 1–4.

de Sio, F. S., Almeida, T., & van den Hoven, J. (2021). The future of work: Freedom, justice and capital in the age of artificial intelligence. *Critical Review of International Social and Political Philosophy.* https://doi.org/10.1080/13698230.2021.2008204.

Dermawan, A. (2023). Text and data mining exceptions in the development of generative AI Models: What the EU member states could learn from the Japanese 'Nonenjoyment' purposes? *The Journal of World Intellectual Property.* https://doi.org/10.1111/jwip.12285.

Dornis, T. W. (2020). Artificial creativity: Emergent works and the void in current copyright doctrine. *Yale Journal of Law & Technology, 22*, 1–60.

Drott, E. (2021). Copyright, compensation, and commons in the music AI industry. *Creative Industries Journal, 14*(2), 190–207.

Dumont, D. (2022). Universal basic income as a source of inspiration for the future of social protection systems? A counter-agenda. *European Journal of Social Security, 24*(4), 299–318.

Engström, V. (2019). Unpacking the debate on social protection floors. *Göttingen Journal of International Law, 9*(3), 571–599.

Etzioni, A. (2017). Job collapse on the road to New Athens. *Challenge, 60*(4), 327–346.

Fouksman, E., & Klein, E. (2019). Radical transformation of technological intervention? Two paths for universal basic income. *World Development*, *122*, 492–500.

Furman, J., & Seamans, R. (2019). AI and the economy. *Innovation Policy and the Economy*, *19*, 161–191.

Geiger, C., & Iaia, V. (2024). The forgotten creator: Towards a statutory remuneration right for machine learning of generative AI. *Computer Law & Security Review: The International Journal of Technology Law and Practice*, *52*, 1–9.

Geiger, C., Schönherr, F., & Jütte, B. J. (2024). *Limitation-based remuneration rights as a compromise between access and remuneration interests in copyright law: What role for collective rights management?* https://papers.ssrn.com/sol3/papers.cfm?abstract_id=4714080

Gervais, D. (2019). The economics of collective management. In B. Depoorter, P. Menel, & D. Schwartz (Eds.), *Research handbook on the economics of intellectual property law, volume 1: Theory* (pp. 489–507). Edward Elgar.

Goldblatt, B. (2020). Basic income, gender and human rights. *University of Oxford Human Rights Hub Journal*, *2020*(1), 68–94.

Haglin, K., Jordan, S., & Ferguson, G. (2023). They're coming for you! How perceptions of automation affect public support for universal basic income. *Social Science Computer Review*. https://doi.org/10.1177/08944393231212252.

Harris, N. (2023). Critical theory and universal basic income. *Critical Sociology*, *49*(7–8), 1141–1156.

Heikkilä, M. (2022, December 16). Artists can now opt out of the next version of stable diffusion. *MIT Technology Review*. www.technologyreview.com/2022/12/16/1065247/artists-can-now-opt-out-of-the-next-version-of-stable-diffusion/.

Hertzmann, A. (2018). Can computers create art? *Arts*, *7*, 1–25.

Hines, A. (2019). Getting ready for a post-work future. *Foresight and STI Governance*, *13*(1), 19–30.

Howcroft, D., & Taylor, P. (2023). Automation and the future of work: A social shaping of technology approach. *New Technology, Work and Employment*, *38*, 351–370.

Jacobsen, B. N. (2023). Machine learning and the politics of synthetic data. *Big Data & Society*. https://doi.org/10.1177/20539517221145372.

Kabasakal Arat, Z. F., & Waring, D. (2022). Rethinking work, the right to work, and automation. *Journal of Human Rights*, *21*(1), 56–72.

Keller, P., & Warso, Z. (2023, September 29). Defining best practices for opting out of ML training. *Open Future Policy Brief No. 5*, https://openfuture.eu/wp-content/uploads/2023/09/Best-_practices_for_optout_ML_training.pdf.

Kelly, K. (2022, November 17). Picture limitless creativity at your fingertips. *Wired*. www.wired.com/story/picture-limitless-creativity-ai-image-generators/.

Kozák, M. (2021). Cultural productivism and public support for the universal basic income from a cross-national perspective. *European Societies*, *23*(1), 23–45.

Lamchek, J. (2020). The right to benefit from big data progress: Another argument for universal basic income. *Völkerrechtsblog*. https://doi.org/10.17176/20200608-133439-0.

Leisering, L. (2020). The calls for universal social protection by international organizations: Constructing a new global consensus. *Social Inclusion, 8*(1), 90–102.

Lim, D. (2018). AI & IP: Innovation creativity in an age of accelerated change. *Akron Law Review, 52*(3), 813–876.

Manza, J. (2023). If universal basic income is the answer, what is the question? *Theory and Society, 52*, 625–639.

Marks, S. P. (2022). Poverty in international human rights. In D. Moeckli, S. Shah, & S. Sivakumaran (Eds.), *International human rights law* (4th ed., pp. 622–643). Oxford University Press.

Merkley, R. (2023, February 27). On AI-generated works, artists, and intellectual property. *Lawfare*. www.lawfaremedia.org/article/ai-generated-works-artists-and-intellectual-property.

Naqvi, Z. (2020). Artificial intelligence, copyright, and copyright infringement. *Marquette Intellectual Property Law Review, 24*(1), 15–52.

Nolan, B. (2022, October 17). Artists say AI image generators are copying their style to make thousands of new images – and it's completely out of their control. *Business Insider*. www.businessinsider.com/ai-image-generators-artists-copying-style-thousands-images-2022-10.

Perkins, G., et al. (2022). Analysing the impacts of universal basic income in the changing world of work: Challenges to the psychological contract and a future research agenda. *Human Resources Management Journal, 32*, 1–18.

Peukert, C. (2019). The next wave of digital technological change and the cultural industries. *Journal of Cultural Economics, 43*, 189–210.

Potts, J. (2023). *The near-death of the author: Creativity in the internet age.* The University of Toronto Press.

Priest, E. (2021). The future of music copyright collectives in the digital streaming age. *Columbia Journal of Law & the Arts, 45*(1), 1–46.

Reagle, J. M. (2019). *Hacking life: Systematized living and its discontents.* The MIT Press.

Rincón, L., Vlandas, T., & Hiilamo, H. (2022). What's not to like? Benefit design, funding structure and support for universal basic income. *Journal of European Social Policy, 32*(4), 467–483.

Selvadurai, N., & Matulionyte, R. (2020). Copyright protection for works generated using artificial intelligence. *Journal of Intellectual Property Law & Practice, 15*(7), 536–543.

Senftleben, M. (2023). Generative AI and author remuneration. *IIC – International Review of Intellectual Property and Competition Law, 54*, 1535–1560.

Simms, M. (2019). *The future of work.* SAGE.

Škiljić, A. (2021). When art meets technology or vice versa: Key challenges at the crossroads of AI-generated artworks and copyright law. *IIC – International Review of Intellectual Property and Competition Law, 52*, 1338–1369.

Sobel, B. L. W. (2017). Artificial intelligence's fair use crisis. *Columbia Journal of Law & the Arts*, *41*(1), 45–98.

Spencer, D. A. (2023). Technology and work: Past lessons and future directions. *Technology in Society*, *74*, 1–7.

Srnicek, N. and Williams, A. (2015). *Inventing the Future: Postcapitalism and a World Without Work*. London: Verso.

Straubhaar, T. (2017). On the economics of a universal basic income. *Intereconomics: Review of European Economic Policy*, *52*(2), 74–80.

Tegmark, M. (2017). *Life 3.0: Being human in the age of artificial intelligence*. Penguin Books.

UN Committee on Economic, Social and Cultural Rights (CESCR), General Comment No. 18: The Right to Work (Art. 6 of the Covenant), 6 February 2006, E/C.12/GC/18.

UN Committee on Economic, Social and Cultural Rights (CESCR), General Comment No. 19: The right to social security (Art. 9 of the Covenant), 4 February 2008, E/C.12/GC/19.

UN General Assembly, International Covenant on Economic, Social and Cultural Rights, 16 December 1966, United Nations, Treaty Series, vol. 993.

UN General Assembly, Universal Declaration of Human Rights, 10 December 1948, 217 A (III).

Van Parijs, P. (2004). Basic income: A simple and powerful idea for the twenty-first century'. *Politics & Society*, *32*(1), 7–39.

Waelen, R. (2022). Why AI ethics is a critical theory. *Philosophy & Technology*, *35*(9), 1–16.

Wiggers, K. (2022, November 11). DeviatArt provides a way for artists to opt out of AI generators. *TechCrunch*. https://techcrunch.com/2022/11/11/deviantart-provides-a-way-for-artists-to-opt-out-of-ai-art-generators/.

Legislation

Directive (EU) 2019/790 of the European Parliament and of the Council of 17 April 2019 on Copyright and Related Rights in the Digital Single Market and Amending Directives 96/9/EC and 2001/29/EC.

5 Human Creativity as Part of ESG and CSR

Several aspects need to be underlined when considering the nature of responsible technological innovation. First, it is important to remember that 'technological development is always informed by specific values of specific stakeholders', and consequently, the nature of implementation can have significant implications on the effects and future directions of technological change; once such implementation already *has* happened, however, changing the course of technological change becomes extremely difficult, if not entirely impossible (de Sio et al., 2021, pp. 6–7). For these reasons, it is crucial to consider not only the status quo of technological innovation or its alternatives but also the rules and norms that would proactively shape the behaviour of actors in the technological innovation ecosystem. In the case of artistic creativity, setting norms pertaining to the role (and potentially, protection) of human authors is particularly relevant. As might be expected, however, the nature and content of such norms and the motivation for organisations to engage in ethical practices raise notable problems. Nevertheless, it is still crucial to explore the ways in which companies using AI technology for creative outputs may, through self-regulation in accordance with ethical standards, support and contribute to the preservation of human creativity and human skills within the arts and creative industries.

5.1 Corporate Social and Digital Responsibility

As argued throughout this book, the latest iteration of AI has definitely moved beyond the mere automation of menial jobs and is now likely to affect the job market in the knowledge and creative sectors. This, in turn, will threaten the livelihood of the broadly conceived creative class (see, e.g., Vithayathil & Nauroth, 2023). Under such circumstances, disengagement from the wider stakes of technology and its application is one of the greatest threats that contemporary societies are facing (Buhmann & Fieseler, 2023) as the challenges and potential downsides of technological innovation remain unaddressed. By contrast, being engaged in responsible innovation is typically seen in terms of living up to 'a challenge embedded in complex and globalized business

DOI: 10.4324/9781003464976-5

environments' (Buhmann & Fieseler, 2023, p. 156), including efforts to ensure the preservation of human creativity as a viable domain of activity. Indeed, some companies have already taken measures in this direction, such as not only embracing generative AI but also setting up funds to compensate authors whose works have been included in training datasets (Heaven, 2022).

One way of ensuring this norm-based approach to innovation is to focus on corporate social responsibility (CSR). CSR is often framed as a way for companies to demonstrate their community engagement and concern for the well-being of the relevant stakeholders and the environment in which the company operates (Triswanto, 2023, p. 37). This extends beyond day-to-day business activities and encompasses broader strategies of impact mitigation and benefit sharing. Instead of being isolating actors engaged in zero-sum games, socially responsible organisations are seen to acknowledge the need for collaboration to produce public goods (Buhmann & Fieseler, 2023, p. 155). Hence, CSR is essentially about addressing the ways for an organisation to become 'a better corporate citizen' (Chang & Ke, 2023, p. 4). CSR has traditionally been seen as a more flexible alternative to large-scale regulation and one that can adapt to changes depending on the time, region, cultural and political realities, and other variables (Argandoña & von Weltzien Hoivik, 2009), including, following this logic, adaptation to the new digital-first realities. Moreover, it is important to have regard for the fact that bottom-up CSR measures tend to be more likely to succeed as research shows that employees bear greater influence than the management on driving the measures to success, thereby increasing the authenticity of such initiatives (Borghesi, 2018).

A key premise here is that 'stakeholder relationships should extend beyond mere compliance with laws and regulations' but should instead be premised upon relationships of mutual care and directed towards the growth of all of those participating so that the actors involved cannot hide behind mere compliance and box-ticking exercises (Boeken, 2024, p. 3; see also Buhmann & Fieseler, 2023, p. 156). Broadly speaking, CSR includes meeting societal expectations and contributing towards the generalised well-being of society at large while also being transparent about the progress made (Hou et al., 2019) and ensuring that business practices are sustainable both societally and environmentally, especially with the rapid pace of digital innovation and development in mind (Pappas et al., 2023). Very similarly, the essence of CSR is defined by Zhuang and Wu (2023, p. 2) as 'environmental impact, ethical responsibility, philanthropic endeavors and financial responsibilities'. However, there is a clearly noticeable lacuna in such accounts, namely, a lack of specificity in terms of human-digital interaction.

Technological transformations, which are fundamental to the functioning of contemporary society, also cannot escape the attention of CSR, at least in terms of the need to give greater attention to the interplays and interdependencies between societal and technological factors to better understand their mutual effects (Heyder et al., 2023, p. 26). Specifically regarding AI, key areas of social responsibility could be seen to include 'transparency, robustness, fairness, equality, respect for human rights, human agency and autonomy as well as data confidentiality' (Chang & Ke, 2023, p. 20), although any such list is not exhaustive. Another key issue identified is 'the importance of bringing ethics to a strategic level in the organization, making the workforce more literate to deal with AI in an ethical way' (Heyder et al., 2023, p. 26). To achieve this, organisations need to put ethics at the forefront to address human-AI interaction in the context of AI's 'increased performance, autonomy, acceptance, and quality' and to integrate 'different stakeholder views to achieve a holistic view of ethics' (Heyder et al., 2023, p. 26). That is, CSR should constitute an all-encompassing framework.

A dividing line is sometimes drawn between Industry 4.0, presented as reckless automation, and Industry 5.0, or humane (perhaps even human-centric) automation, with Industry 5.0 aiming to 'reset the economic and social balance through responsible governance' (Asif et al., 2023, p. 1). Broadly speaking, the focus is thus on making 'transitioning towards a digital society' and sustainability (both societal and environmental) mutually compatible (Asif et al., 2023, p. 1). Increasingly, there is an awareness that economic success taken in isolation cannot be the sole criterion in evaluating the performance of an organisation, particularly if such success leads to social consequences that are unsustainable in the broad sense of the term; consequently, the imperative is that 'firms must leverage advanced technologies to create workplaces that are human-centered, benefit society, and improve quality of life' (Asif et al., 2023, p. 1). Although the premise here is definitely correct, one might be somewhat sceptical about the progressivist imperative to use technology for problem-solving. In fact, care in the deployment (and sometimes not engaging in the full deployment) of digital technologies might yield more societally sustainable results.

A characteristic argument here is that a greater adoption of more innovative technology equals more advanced business models, which equals greater value for society (see, e.g., Asif et al., 2023). This should be seen as a reiteration of the typical progressivist argument that a transition to new technologies will be traumatic only to those who are unable to embrace change and adapt to changing environments, while those agile enough will benefit from immense and transformative opportunities (see, e.g., Vithayathil & Nauroth, 2023, p. 263). In fact, AI and related technologies are even being touted as *enablers* of CSR allegedly by helping to address and manage stakeholder issues (Zhuang & Wu, 2023). Some authors would go as far as adopting a view that could be called utopian determinism, namely, that technology itself is bound to lead to a more normatively desirable life: as Vithayathil and Nauroth (2023, p. 263) claim, 'new opportunities will be far greater than those eliminated by the inexorable advance of AI'; that is, there might be pain in the short run but immense societal gain in the long-term perspective. Thus, CSR initiatives can easily get mired in the concentration on short-term transition management because long-term benefits will quasi-magically sort themselves out. Likewise, such a utopian determinist picture of ever-increasing progress is almost unavoidably expanded to also encompass ever-growing equality: '[f]rom any point on the globe, software and algorithm developers today and tomorrow have seamless access to a breath of technologies required to build even more powerful AI' (Vithayathil & Nauroth, 2023, p. 264). Unfortunately, such assertions are only possible by completely ignoring material and access inequalities, market concentration in the technology sector, and systemic disadvantages in the global economy. Therefore, it is crucial not only that CSR measures are in place but also that the overly naïve versions of these measures are precluded.

To focus more specifically on the impact of digital technologies, Lobschat et al., (2021, p. 876) specifically emphasise corporate digital responsibility (CDR) as a special field of consideration geared towards 'ensuring the ethical design and uses of digital technologies and related data' by way of companies developing 'a comprehensive, coherent set of norms, embedded in their organizational culture, to govern the development and deployment of digital technology and data' as informed by shared norms and values. The onus is therefore on corporate actors to ensure that their practices reflect a core set of concerns around how 'the code they produce or deploy, as well as data they collect and process, inherently create an ethical responsibility for them' (Lobschat et al., 2021, p. 876). Similarly in the broader CSR framework, CDR refers to 'a voluntarily established set of policies and self-governing principles, developed, implemented, and overseen by corporations themselves' that go beyond formal regulations (van der Merwe & Al Achkar, 2022, p. 4). However, there is also a notable difference in that 'CDR focuses on unprecedented risks and obstacles of (digital) technologies rather than the relatively broad goal of CSR concerning society where technology plays only a subordinate role' (Carl et al., 2023, p. 7; see also Mihale-Wilson et al., 2022, pp. 128–129). At stake here is 'the explicit consideration of the digital, beyond an organization's wider social responsibility' (Lobschat et al., 2021, p. 876). Elsewhere, CDR is presented as almost a silver bullet that can solve societal, political, economic, and environmental problems by simply adhering to a set of ethical commitments (see, e.g., Elliott et al., 2021).

The scope of CDR is often taken to be very broad indeed by encompassing the impact of digital transformation on individuals, societies, states, the environment, etc. (see, e.g., van der Merwe & Al Achkar, 2022, p. 5). Elsewhere, the key stakeholders are identified as individuals, organisations, governmental and other institutions, and the technological actors themselves (see, e.g., Lobschat et al., 2021; Herden et al., 2021). Nevertheless, even despite the mentioning of the impact on individuals, there is almost universally nothing written about employees or the impact on human employment more broadly – just the mantra of retraining and the general reshaping of work. Meanwhile, insofar as individuals are concerned, the focus is typically on the audience/consumer-facing human impact, such as privacy or manipulation. It is illustrative that, for example, Herden et al. (2021), who identified 20 groups of issues that CDR is supposed to address, do not manage to dedicate at least one of these groups to employment or other issues pertaining to remunerating humans for their activities. A more occupational-focused take on CDR is offered by Trier et al. (2023, p. 468) who emphasise ways in which '[o]rganizational environments . . . create new social and psychological demands for employees and lead to changing conditions', such as increased digital availability pressures, algorithmic management, etc. The concentration is nevertheless still on occupational transformation rather than on occupational displacement and the changing conditions of work rather than on changing the availability of work altogether. Hence, transformations of employment and remuneration structures are at best captured within broad ideas, such as the respect for human dignity and autonomy being placed at the heart of corporate responsibility (Wirtz et al., 2023, p. 174).

The challenge here is ensuring that alignment with human values and progress towards sustainable development are central to business practices and not merely treated as a means towards other aims (e.g., responsibility as merely a tool to earn larger profits). Instead, corporate responsibility must be an end in itself, that is, responsibility should take precedence regardless of its effect on the bottom line. As Chang and Ke (2023, p. 4) put it, organisations 'ought to be responsible not only for their bottom line but also for those who contribute to the bottom line, namely, the environment, community, and society' (Chang & Ke, 2023, p. 4). Notably, however, some existing research indicates that responsibility and business performance could be, in fact, complementary, namely, greater social responsibility correlates with more traditional measures of business performance, including in the creative industries (Hou et al., 2019, p. 276). Indeed, being able to demonstrate ethical commitments while also making use of available technological and other growth opportunities is a key asset and might lead to win-win scenarios, particularly in terms of increased trust among both shareholders and consumers (Zhuang & Wu, 2023).

Broadly speaking, CDR approaches can be classified into those 'focused on the avoidance of negative consequences', on the one hand, and 'those that employ CDR in efforts to establish and pursue a competitively relevant positioning in the market' (Mueller, 2022, p. 697), on the other hand, but neither of these come to be motivated by logics other than business performance narrowly conceived. Specifically, CDR becomes more of a means rather than an end and raises issues as to the motivation to engage in such measures and to do so openly. For any responsibility frameworks to have any impact, robust transparency measures must be put in place or otherwise, the efficiency of any normative frameworks would be limited. As Moodaley and Telukdarie (2023) underscore, the inflation of sustainability claims – commonly known as greenwashing – is already plaguing CSR and CDR. If the human-focused adoption of generative AI becomes the norm, then something akin to human-washing (such as inflating the role of humans within the creative processes) would likely follow. No less importantly, within the domain of AI, ensuring performance in line with CSR and CDR practices needs to be a permanently ongoing process because of the dynamic nature of digital technologies whereby static, ready-made solutions will soon become outdated (Buhmann & Fieseler, 2023, p. 156). This process of constant revision and adaptation is also investment- and labour-intensive, which means that without incentives or enforcement, ethical practice will likely lag behind.

5.2   Towards a Framework for Sustainability-Focused Human Inclusion

Although CSR pertains to a normative commitment, similar concerns can also be addressed in a more utilitarian fashion: for example, the environmental, social, and governance (ESG) framework in investment interprets ethical business practices as a means to mitigate financial risks (Minkkinen et al., 2022). That is, 'ESG Issues are considered *material* – that is, relevant to an asset's future financial performance – thus making their integration into the investment analysis necessary for capturing greater benefits from the investment' (Minkkinen et al., 2022, p. 4). Crucially, if such considerations are applied by a critical mass of investors, then this could act as an informal enforcement mechanism to ensure that companies live up to their responsibilities and commitments. The environmental side of this framework is relatively straightforward, the social side encompasses the organisation's treatment of and impact on its stakeholders, including employees, and the governance part refers to the ways in which an organisation's internal rules and practices contribute to the achievement of equitable outcomes (Minkkinen et al., 2022).

Meanwhile, for other scholars (see, notably, Sætra, 2021), the ESG framework constitutes a more precisely articulated replacement of the rather vague CSR. Likewise, it could be argued that CDR might (as yet) be too abstract to be practically implemented (Mihale-Wilson et al., 2022, p. 131). Still, there are value-based challenges pertaining to the focus of ESG, and it is seen as mostly about the early identification and avoidance of potential pitfalls and controversies so that value-diminishing outcomes can be prevented while growth and return on investment are ensured, thereby losing track of the actual ethical impetus and individual and societal interests. Such progressivist approaches also have a tendency to assume that humans are quasi-determined to be beneficiaries, either by freeing up their time or by retraining (see, characteristically, Brusseau, 2023, p. 1033; a similar outlook regarding only CDR is also expressed by Mueller, 2022). Similarly to CDR, however, occupational, employment, and remuneration issues remain under-addressed: for example, Sætra (2022, p. 1031) reduces employees to a sub-issue of broader social considerations; moreover, in-work challenges of the existing workforce are identified rather than the challenges of the people left out of the emerging AI-focused economy, including individuals involved in the domain of creativity. Simultaneously, what does get acknowledged is 'a need to deal with the economic consequences related to inequality, poverty, access to infrastructure, and so forth under the social dimension of the AI ESG protocol' (Sætra, 2022, p. 1032). In particular, the focus on freeing up time and retraining is ill-suited to artistic creativity where human labour and input is understood (as already shown in this book) to be at the heart of artistic practice as such. Thus, the conventional focus is ill-suited to the challenges faced by human creators and will have to be reframed at the end of this chapter.

Crucially, the ESG framework does not exist in a vacuum – instead, Sætra (2021, 2022) provides a useful classification of the three summands vis-à-vis the Sustainable Development Goals (SDGs), with a specific emphasis on the corporate use of AI. For such purposes, Goals 6 (clean water and sanitation), 7 (affordable and clean energy), 9 (industry, innovation, and infrastructure), 11 (sustainable cities and communities), 12 (responsible consumption and production), 13 (climate action), 14 (life below water), and 15 (life on land) refer to the sustainability part, Goals 1 (no poverty), 2 (zero hunger), 3 (good health and well-being), 4 (quality education), 5 (gender equality), 6 (clean water and sanitation), 8 (decent work and economic growth), 9 (industry, innovation, and infrastructure), 10 (reduced inequalities), 12 (responsible consumption and production), and 16 (peace, justice, and strong institutions) refer to the social part, and Goals 5 (gender equality), 8 (decent work and economic growth), 9 (industry, innovation, and infrastructure), 11 (sustainable cities and communities), 12 (responsible consumption and production), 13 (climate action), 16 (peace, justice, and strong institutions), and 17 (partnerships for the goals) refer to the governance part (see Sætra, 2021, p. 4). For the purposes of this analysis, Goals 5, 8, 9, and 12 are of particular importance, both thematically and because of their cross-cutting nature (with Goals 9 and 12 pertaining to all three aspects of ESG).

In terms of Goal 5 (gender equality), Target 5.5.b, which focuses on technology as a means of empowerment, is of great relevance. Even though its sole indicator is constructed very narrowly (mobile phone ownership), it is reasonable to extend its focus on the disproportionate effect of the digital divide on women. Regarding AI, equal access to technology (not just generative AI models but also connectivity and the necessary hardware) so that women can compete in an increasingly technology-centric environment is key. Within the ambit of this book, access to hardware, sufficient connectivity, and digital creativity tools (including generative models) are paramount. Likewise, it is crucial that remuneration, whether through licencing schemes, universal handouts, certification schemes (laid out in the next chapter), and other means of remuneration are accessible irrespective of gender.

As for Goal 8 (decent work and economic growth), several targets have particular importance: notably, Target 8.5 stipulates the achievement of full and productive employment, while Target 8.8 focuses on labour rights. Although the antinomies between automation and full employment were already laid out in the discussion of UBI and post-work earlier in this book, from an SDG perspective, responsible business practices are implementing technologies (including AI) in a way that do not jeopardise the employment opportunities of human workers (ideally, they also create new possibilities for employment) and do not frame such substitution potential as a bargaining chip to apply downward pressure on labour rights. In fact, it might even be suggested that human quotas be adopted by technology-intensive companies, such as specific amounts of workplaces being reserved for humans in the creative industries, should organisations choose to automate creative processes. Notably, although quotas are generally a controversial concept, they are nonetheless regarded as an effective tool to reduce the systemic barriers that exist due to discrimination, stereotypes, or other forms of a systemic lack of opportunity (Conde-Ruiz et al., 2020). However, this is not without practical difficulties: for example, one thorny issue might be the referent value from which the quota would be derived (potential options might be a pre-automation workforce, the workforce of similar companies that have forfeited automation, etc.).

Nevertheless, transparency reporting, including the information related to the change in human employee numbers engaged in roles that produce creative outputs, could still potentially constitute at least a nudge towards a more human-friendly adoption of generative AI, particularly if these data are contextualised, that is, they are provided with the data relating to the adoption of AI tools for certain tasks or services. It is accepted that in the context of humans and AI, it is not possible to have clear quotas as is the case in the context of, for example, women and men. However, the concept of quotas could comprise different elements to which companies could commit, for example, the decrease in humans employed for creative tasks could not exceed an agreed percentage point. In addition, companies could commit to employing a certain number of humans and link the number with certain performance indicators. Likewise, other companies could take up the responsibility to continue purchasing a proportion of artistic works and creative services from human authors. Still, as previously mentioned, if current reporting issues are to be learned from, 'human-washing' might emerge as a significant concern.

Regarding Goal 9 (industry, innovation, and infrastructure), Target 9.5 emphasises the importance of research and innovation, and Target 9.9.c specifically deals with access to communication technologies. Adopting cutting-edge technologies and developing state-of-the-art tools (including generative AI models) that are made available to the general public are the key to growth in the contemporary economy while connectivity is a necessary condition for making use of these opportunities. Simultaneously, such growth cannot take place at the expense of human authors. Hence, the development of and access to digital technologies should be paired with remuneration strategies, either in terms of the quotas referred to earlier or the measures described in other chapters, such as a guaranteed basic income for human authors. That is, benefits of technological innovation and economic growth should be distributed equitably. Finally, concerning Goal 12 (responsible consumption and production), Target 12.12.a, which concentrates on the technological capacity to transition towards more sustainable production and consumption, is of note, particularly in terms of the need to address the environmental concerns raised by the training of AI models, content generation, and its storage (which again, implies the need to move beyond the target's narrowly framed sole indicator). In this case, the limitation to the training and deployment of AI models would have a simultaneous environmental *and* human impact: such models consume significant amounts of resources (as does the storage of their output), which makes (voluntary) limitations desirable, and this sustainability-focused drive would have a positive impact on the human capacity to compete in a technology-saturated marketplace. Similarly, sustainability could (and, arguably, should) be framed in more than just environmental terms but also regarding the impact on humans. This reasoning could likewise support the (self-)imposition of limitations.

Ultimately, Brusseau (2023, p. 1035) makes a vital observation by emphasising the importance of human dignity, as derived from the Kantian imperative that humans are to be treated as ends in themselves and not merely as a means. In this sense, consumer interest should also be clear. Of course, industry standards and CSR can be drivers of change, but this is especially true when there is consumer pressure (Altenburger, 2018). Nevertheless, purely ethical or utilitarian considerations might be insufficient, not least because the drive behind potential implementation is jeopardised by an apparent lack of consumer awareness of and preference for compliance with corporate responsibility norms (Carl et al., 2023, p. 36). In this situation, referring back to the governance options might re-emerge as a possibility. Here, Elliott et al. (2021), for example, suggest resorting to standardisation networks for support. An alternative option might also be regulation by public institutions so that societal interests are adequately addressed (Trier et al., 2023, p. 471). This, however, undermines the very premise of corporate responsibility measures – namely, as a means to omit the lacunae of legal regulation or go beyond the minimal commitments set out by the law.

As a result, then, neither the commitment by businesses to engage in ethical and sustainable practices nor the effectiveness of any measures thereby put in place can be taken for granted. Likewise, it must be accepted that this cannot be a universal model due to market changes, financial difficulties, or changes in business priorities that indicate that a more drastic transformation in company structure may be required, thus making it difficult to maintain certain commitments for prolonged periods of time. In addition, the model would be difficult to scale because of the differences among business models and the fact that there could be business models based on the complete elimination of humans in the creative tasks as a unique selling point. Still, transparency reporting would be a key element of any self-regulatory measures. Then, individual business commitment to human skill preservation (quotas, tooling, contributions to author support schemes, etc.), as demonstrated against certain performance indicators, could be publicly communicated with progress reports also made available to the public. Arguably, such a mechanism not only could contribute to preserving human creativity and reducing de-skilling or the speed thereof but also would contribute to trust in the business and positively influence better-informed consumer choices. Thus, if incentives are sufficiently stacked, then CDR and ESG measures can be put in place to help mitigate the impact of generative AI on human authors. However, due to both their voluntary nature and limited scope, they cannot alone produce sufficient outcomes to retain incentives for human authors. Instead, they can be effective as part of a wider combination of measures.

Bibliography

Altenburger, R. (2018). Corporate social responsibility as a driver of innovation processes. In R. Altenburger (Ed.), *Innovation management and corporate social responsibility* (pp. 1–12). Springer.

Argandoña, A., & von Weltzien Hoivik, H. (2009). Corporate social responsibility: One size does not fit all. Collecting evidence from Europe. *Journal of Business Ethics, 89*, 221–234.

Asif, M., Searcy, C., & Castka, P. (2023). ESG and industry 5.0: The role of technologies in enhancing ESG disclosure. *Technological Forecasting & Social Change, 195*, 1–12.

Boeken, J. (2024). From compliance to security, responsibility beyond law. *Computer Law & Security Review: The International Journal of Technology Law and Practice, 52*, 1–5.

Borghesi, R. (2018). Employee political affiliation as a driver of corporate social responsibility intensity. *Applied Economics, 50*, 2117–2132.

Brusseau, J. (2023). AI human impact: Toward a model for ethical investing in AI-intensive companies. *Journal of Sustainable Finance & Investment, 13*(2), 1030–1057.

Buhmann, A., & Fieseler, C. (2023). Deep learning meets deep democracy: Deliberative governance and responsible innovation in artificial intelligence. *Business Ethics Quarterly, 33*(1), 146–179.

Carl, C. V., Mihale-Wilson, C., Zibuschka, J., & Hinz, O. (2023). A consumer perspective on corporate digital responsibility: An empirical evaluation of consumer preferences. *Journal of Business Economics.* https://doi.org/10.1007/s11573-023-01142-y.

Chang, Y. L., & Ke, J. (2023). Socially responsible artificial intelligence empowered people analytics: A novel framework towards sustainability. *Human Resource Development Review.* https://doi.org/10.1177/15344843231200930.

Conde-Ruiz, J. I., García, M., & Yáñez, M. (2020). Does a 'soft' board gender quotas policy work? *Applied Economic Analysis*, *28*, 46–68.

de Sio, F. S., Almeida, T., & van den Hoven, J. (2021). The future of work: Freedom, justice and capital in the age of artificial intelligence. *Critical Review of International Social and Political Philosophy*. https://doi.org/10. 1080/13698230.2021.2008204.

Elliott, K. Price, R., Shaw, P., Spiliotopoulos, T., Ng, M., Coopamootoo, K., & van Moorsel, A. (2021). Towards an equitable digital society: Artificial Intelligence (AI) and Corporate Digital Responsibility (CDR). *Society*, *58*, 179–188.

Heaven, W. D. (2022, December 16). Generative AI Is changing everything. But what's left when the hype is gone? *MIT Technology Review*. www. technologyreview.com/2022/12/16/1065005/generative-ai-revolution-art/.

Herden, C. J., Alliu, E., Cakici, A., Cormier, T., Deguelle, C., Gambhir, S., Griffiths, C., Gupta, S., Kamani, S. R., Kiratli, Y.-S., Kispataki, M., Lange, G., Moles de Matos, L., Tripero Moreno, L., Betancourt Nunez, H. A., Pilla, V., Raj, B., Roe, J., Skoda, M., Song, Y., Ummadi, P. K., & Edinger-Schons, L. M. (2021). Corporate digital responsibility: New corporate responsibilities in the digital age. *Nachhaltigkeits/Management Forum*, *29*, 13–29.

Heyder, T., Passlack, N., & Posegga, O. (2023). Ethical management of human-AI interaction: Theory development review. *Journal of Strategic Information Systems*, *32*, 1–50.

Hou, C. E., Lu, W. M., & Hung, S. W. (2019). Does CSR matter? Influence of corporate social responsibility on corporate performance in the creative industry. *Annals of Operations Research*, *278*, 255–279.

Lobschat, L., et al. (2021). Corporate digital responsibility. *Journal of Business Research*, *122*, 875–888.

Mihale-Wilson, C., et al. (2022). Corporate digital responsibility. *Business Information Systems Engineering*, *64*, 127–132.

Minkkinen, M., Niukkanen, A., & Mäntimäki, M. (2022). What about investors? ESG analyses as tools foe ethics-based AI auditing. *AI & Society*. https://doi.org/10.1007/s00146-022-01415-0.

Moodaley, W., & Telukdarie, A. (2023). Greenwashing, sustainability reporting, and artificial intelligence: A systematic literature review. *Sustainability*, *15*, 1–25.

Mueller, B. (2022). Corporate digital responsibility. *Business Information Systems Engineering*, *64*, 689–700.

Pappas, I. O., et al. (2023). Responsible digital transformation for a sustainable society. *Information Systems Frontiers*, *25*, 245–253.

Sætra, H. S. (2021). A framework for evaluating and disclosing the ESG related impacts of AI with the SDGs. *Sustainability*, *13*, 1–16.

Sætra, H. S. (2022). The AI ESG protocol: Evaluating and disclosing the environment, social, and governance implications of artificial intelligence capabilities, assets, and activities. *Sustainable Development*, *31*, 1037–1037.

Trier, M., Kundisch, D., Beverungen, D., Müller, O., Schryen, G., Mirbabaie, M., & Trang, S. (2023). Digital responsibility: A multilevel framework for responsible digitalization. *Business Information Systems Engineering*, *65*, 463–474.

Triswanto, T. S. (2023). Business ethics and social ethics in Corporate Social Responsibility (CSR) in the 4.0 Industrial revolution. *International Journal of Economics, Management, Business and Social Sciences*, *3*(1), 36–41.

van der Merwe, J., & Al Achkar, Z. (2022). Data responsibility, corporate social responsibility, and corporate digital responsibility. *Data & Policy*, *4*, 1–12.

Vithayathil, J., & Nauroth, M. (2023). The brave new world of artificial intelligence. *Journal of Global Information Technology Management*, *26*(4), 261–268.

Wirtz, J., et al. (2023). Corporate digital responsibility in service firms and their ecosystems. *Journal of Service Research*, *26*(2), 173–190.

Zhuang, X., & Wu, Y. (2023). ChatGPT: How it can support corporate social responsibility. *Journal of Business Strategy*. https://doi.org/10.1108/JBS-05-2023-0089.

6   Designations and Strengthening Consumer Protection – To the Rescue of Human Authors

The final option discussed in this book is the creation of certification schemes for creative works to prove their human provenance. Inspiration here is taken from Geographical Indications (GIs), namely, that by linking a product to a particular location (typically referred to as a *terroir*), two important purposes are served. First, GIs are intended to protect the interests of producers by establishing and confirming the exclusivity of their product by maintaining exclusivity and therefore enabling a premium price. Second, GIs help protect consumer interests as sources of important information about the purchased product and its specificities. Although not without their critics (as shown in the following), GIs therefore act as important carriers of information and facilitators of commercial interactions. Hence, after discussing the likely consumer preferences in the domain of artistic creativity and AI-generated content (the purported consumer interests to be protected) and the basic provisions of GIs, this chapter concludes with a discussion of what Human Indications (HIs) could potentially look like and what their benefits and drawbacks would likely be.

6.1   Is There a Consumer Interest to Be Protected?

The first task in this chapter is to establish whether there is a clearly defined consumer interest to be protected and if so, what challenges arise vis-à-vis generative AI. Here, notably, a marked condition of the art market is its socially constructed nature, whereby the value of artistic works is not intrinsic but instead results from cultural, aesthetic, economic, and other considerations that not only pertain to the individual but also, perhaps even more importantly, are of a collective nature (Velthuis, 2013). Cultural goods function in society as 'experience goods' (Peukert, 2019, p. 199); this means that instead of objective value, the focus is always on perceived value, which arises from a combination of personal preferences, on the one hand, and peer influence on the other hand, with both also changing over time. Indeed, both the notion and the value of creativity are hotly contested matters; they encompass the full

DOI: 10.4324/9781003464976-6

spectrum from completely individualistic to societally and environmentally embedded considerations and interpretations (Wingström et al., 2022).

Likewise, the value of AI-generated output, instead of being intrinsic, is conditional on prior expectations and pre-existing convictions about the origi- nator of the work in question (Hong et al., 2021). After all, it is one thing to arrange pixels, notes, words, or other structural elements in a way recognis- able by humans and reminiscent to the way that humans would arrange them; it is still another thing to induce the process of the object's emergence as a meaningful work of art through a 'networked interaction *between* multiple people and objects' (Bown, 2021, p. 9). A framework to be broadly followed here is Audry and Ippolito's (2019) embrace of a Foucauldian perspective; they argue for an audience-centric approach to evaluate AI creativity (and, therefore, the potential challenge to human authors), assuming that significant shifts in the arts market are only possible in conjunction with a comparable change in audience tastes and opinions. Therefore, it seems relatively uncon- troversial that when it comes to the practical impact that AI-generated art might end up having on the art market, it is not formal definitions of creativity but instead, folk perceptions and public reactions that matter (Mikalonytė & Kneer, 2022). Indeed, when thinking about the potential impact of AI on the livelihood of and incentives for human artists, it is the purchase and consump- tion intention of the audience that should be seen as the key deciding factor.

In addition, Cohen (2007) develops a rather nuanced model of creativity, which is relevant here. She sees creativity as rather humble and non-inde- pendent and characterised by not knowing the result in advance but instead being situated within and being affected by (and simultaneously affecting in return) one's own temporal cultural context that enables or disables particular creative opportunities (Cohen, 2007, p. 1178). Creativity is also dependent upon equally situated users who not only determine the horizon of acceptabil- ity but also are pushed themselves by new works; this also ties in with the key role that time- and culture-specific demands, practices, and paradigms play in determining the scope of artistic expression (Cohen, 2007, pp. 1179–1183). The horizon of possibility thus established is, of course, not immutable, which means that boundary crossing is a constant part of artistic practice (Cohen, 2007, p. 1187), leading to the possibility of experimentation and productive juxtaposition (Cohen, 2007, p. 1190). Considering AI-generated content and its impact on human authors, such a situatedness-focused view is a rather open one, identifying the author as enmeshed in cultural practices (as gen- erative AI tools are because of their data-centric nature) who is constantly pushing and being pushed back by existing boundaries (which is possible as AI recombines training data). The most problematic aspect here would likely again be the audience impact – to adequately appreciate content and partake in horizon-setting, individuals need to know what exactly they encounter and to formulate their preferences accordingly.

There may, of course, also be additional benefits of human-created art-works, independent of their artistic value. Notably, art can and often does perform a social and political function by pinpointing the defects and short-comings in societies and human relationships while suggesting a way forward or offering cautionary visions of the future; meanwhile, AI-generated output can only, at best, mimic such concern but without penetrating the fabric of human societies – after all, AI does not experience and is not affected by social and political conditions in the way that humans are (Senftleben, 2023, p. 1538). The lack of experience and reliance on mere mimicked knowledge also means that both the present condition and the historical record of human societies can be distortedly represented in both allegedly factual and artistic works (Makhortykh et al., 2023). The relative importance of such considera-tions, however, is yet again premised upon the dominant societal expectations of what an artwork is or should be and what function it is to perform (e.g., socially engaged art versus art for its own sake).

If we understand creativity as a social phenomenon (see generally Bown, 2021), then not only creative actors, processes, and artefacts matter but also the audiences, their inputs (such as dominant tastes, willingness to pay, etc.), and their perceptions upon which such inputs are premised matter. This inter-active approach has a major implication, namely, that no understanding of what counts as creativity and art is final but is instead in a constant process of change and development. Therefore, no current constellation (including potential scepticism as to the art-ness of AI-generated content) should be taken as final or disqualifying, even though existing attitudes do shape aesthetic and market conditions under which current artistic developments take place and future directions are being shaped. Accordingly, even if consumer interests can be established at least in broad terms, they must be taken as a snapshot within an ever-evolving process and not as final and set in stone. In addition, the idea of creativity as a social phenomenon underscores the importance of transparency (e.g., as to whether a particular item has been produced by a human author or by AI): if the interaction that socially shapes creativity and art-ness is to carry on unobstructed, it is crucial that all parties involved have full and accurate information so that any developments represent their stance and authentic input. For this reason, although particular consumer preferences may be transient, transparency must be understood as the more enduring part of consumer interest.

Of course, complete human-centricity cannot be presumed due to the growing importance of 'collaborative filtering' in determining the popular-ity of digital content, where collaboration involves both human-human and human-algorithm interactions in driving or throttling the popularity and spread of a particular item (Peukert, 2019). Human choices and algorithmic content moderation both play a role in this process and do so interactively: human choices are informed by algorithmic content selection while such selection rests on machine learning human preferences. Hence, the prominence (and, consequently, perceived value) of digital items arises from this interaction. Nevertheless, there is still, for now, one area of this interaction where human-ascribed value counts: as Veale and Pérez y Pérez (2020) observe, at least until there is no market in machines purchasing and enjoying machine-generated goods (if ever such a market is to emerge at all), it is human appreciation and the value perceived by humans that counts, which makes it also worthwhile to delve into *human* consumer interests. This is not to say that such meaning and value emergence is a straightforward process – instead, there is a real possibility that '[e]xtreme content abundance . . . will inundate us with noise, and we'll need to find new techniques and strategies to manage the deluge' (De Cremer et al., 2023). It is thus reasonable to expect that the ability to identify human-created works within this deluge of content would allow them to command a premium (De Cremer et al., 2023), implying the need for certification and other provenance-establishment schemes.

The need for establishing provenance rests on the assumed wisdom that audiences, at least for now, tend to value AI-generated output less than human-created art (see, e.g., Hong & Curran, 2019; Sun et al., 2023). Although some would deride such attitudes as 'Luddite' and, therefore, by implication, backwardly (see, e.g., Chung, 2023), the audience relationship with AI-generated content is definitely more complex than a mere resistance to (technological) change. For example, Tubadji et al. (2021, p. 2) propose an evolutionary mechanism to explain this propensity, namely, an inclination towards 'favouring cultural proximity in economic choice, which stimulates a "home bias" in consumer choice'. It is this cultural proximity between the creators and the consumers of goods that is seen to give rise to the preference of human-created works, thereby demonstrating the importance of subjective and cultural economic values.

Empirical research suggests that there is a correlation between individuals' anthropocentric beliefs about creativity and a lower opinion of AI-generated outputs on both cognitive and emotional levels (i.e., lower ascription of creativity and lower appreciation); this might be the result of human-motivated reasoning (an unwillingness to admit information contrary to one's beliefs), as Millet et al. (2023) suggest, but this would still likely have very real consequences on purchase intention and the price one is willing to pay. Similar results are also reported by Fortuna and Modliński (2021), with their participants both manifesting lesser appreciation and intending to pay a lower price for AI-generated artwork (for a broader conceptual elaboration, see also Messingschlager & Appel, 2023). Even in cases where extrinsic motivations, such as benevolent intentions, are obvious (such as charitable giving ads), the awareness of content being AI-generated has a negative impact on perceived authenticity, audience engagement, and financial commitment (Arango et al., 2023). For this reason, it is important that consumers have sufficient knowledge about the origin of the work when making their purchase decisions.

Interestingly, however, such human-centric beliefs can be manipulated: for example, anthropomorphising the AI system (e.g., giving it at least a virtual human face, providing a back story, etc.) can increase the acceptance and ascribed value of AI-generated output (Sun et al., 2023). Likewise, experimental evidence seems to indicate that human reaction to and treatment of AI-generated output depend on the framing: although there is at least some degree of anthropocentricity in the default perception, the descriptions used in presenting such output, including the use of linguistic cues (again, primarily in terms of anthropomorphising AI), can nudge audiences into perceiving greater agency and, therefore, more value in AI-generated content (Epstein et al., 2020). In this context, interesting findings are presented by Moura and Maw (2021) who note an ostensible gap between attitudes towards and actual evaluations of AI-generated content: their participants displayed a negative bias towards AI creativity in general, but when asked to evaluate AI-generated music, they tended to evaluate it on par with human-created samples. Similarly, Mikalonytė and Kneer's (2022) research participants, although intuiting that AI lacks qualities typically associated with creativity, nevertheless did not evaluate AI-generated paintings as being of lower quality than human-created ones.

However, whatever their attitudes, individuals often struggle to correctly identify AI-generated works and instead often resort to stereotypes of what *they think* AI-generated works could be like, with samples stretching across painting (Gangadharbatla, 2022; see also Mazzone & Elgammal, 2019; Ornes, 2019; Park et al., 2023) and text (Köbis & Mossink, 2021; Hitsuwari et al., 2023). For example, Ornes (2019, p. 4761) reports that participants in an experiment even tended to unwittingly prefer AI-generated works in terms of them 'being more novel, complex, and surprising' than human-created ones. Meanwhile, Gangadharbatla's (2022) research suggests an inability of humans to distinguish between artworks created by machines and those created by humans, albeit with some intrinsic biases, such as more readily ascribing representative works to humans and abstract ones to computers (see also Hitsuwari et al., 2023; Tigre Moura et al., 2023). Another biased pattern was observed by Köbis and Mossink (2021) whose research participants showed significantly greater acceptance of AI generating newspaper articles than poetry. Nevertheless, the same participants not only struggled to separate AI-written from human-written poetry but also did not experience a notable drop in their evaluations after being post hoc informed of the algorithmic origin of poetic texts (Köbis & Mossink, 2021, p. 10). Elsewhere, Tigre Moura and Maw (2021: 144), when studying music perception, found that there was no significant relationship between awareness of the origin of a particular piece and its perception, with listeners providing favourable representations even in cases where they had initially been sceptical about artificial creativity.

Meanwhile, Peukert (2019, p. 206) indicates that there might well be a demand-side preference for a human touch that would preclude a total replacement of human artists with machines. In line with this argument, some existing research suggests that humans do ascribe lower aesthetic value to AI-generated art regardless of their knowledge of authorship or lack thereof (see, e.g., Hong & Curran, 2019). Likewise, existing (admittedly limited) data suggest that people may be willing to pay less for AI creations than for human ones regardless of the perceived aesthetic or artistic value (Fortuna & Modliński, 2021). In contrast, Gangadharbatla (2022) implies a more nuanced picture: in line with the previously outlined aesthetic ascriptions, the knowledge of AI's creative input did reduce purchase intentions for representational artworks, but this effect was also observed for abstract ones. However, AI content generation has a significant advantage over human-created artistic works: even in cases when the average output is not particularly successful, it costs almost nothing to repeat the generation process multiple times until a standout piece appears (Hoel, 2021), which means that even if a relatively low percentage of outputs is perceived by the audience as worthwhile, this still provides a good enough commercial opportunity for those wielding creative AI agents while significantly harming the interests of human authors who only have one try at a time.

Therefore, although the evidence is mixed, this does not in itself reduce the need for transparency. On the contrary, as noted earlier, transparency is crucial not only for those who tend to prefer human-created works but also for those who are more indifferent as to the origin of content since it enables the shaping of the arts market in line with societal attitudes. Nevertheless, transparency is particularly important to ensure that individuals who choose to acquire or otherwise enjoy human-created works or to pay a premium price for such works have sufficient information when making their purchase decisions. Generally, transparency is already framed as a key necessity for ensuring effective human-AI collaboration and something that needs to be confirmed through joint efforts by governments and technology companies (Nah et al., 2023). Nevertheless, although the innovation potential of generative AI is beyond doubt, the introduction and maintenance of ethics standards, including guidelines for transparency, prove to be problematic (Banh & Strobel, 2023). Regarding (generative) AI, transparency is typically understood in terms of *how* decisions are made or content is generated (see, e.g., Banh & Strobel, 2023; Ooi et al., 2023). However, this is not enough – more attention needs to also be given to *what* has been generated (the transparency requirements set out in Article 52 of the EU AI Act signal a notable step in this direction).

There is already a strong drive towards transparency in domains outside art, for example, in the context of academic research, whereby credibility and integrity are seen to rest on transparency (see, e.g., Kostygina et al., 2023; Tang et al., 2023). Moreover, transparency not only is important for maintaining integrity but also empowers the audience in terms of enabling individuals to evaluate and remain in control of their content consumption choices (Tang et al., 2023). In this context, Park et al. (2023) propose the use of AI tools to identify content generated by other AI tools to support better-informed audience decisions. Nevertheless, it is also the case that differentiating between AI-generated (or hybrid human and AI) content and that created by humans remains a steep task, including for purpose-built tools (see, e.g., BaHammam, 2023; Hodges & Kirschner, 2024; Williams, 2024), let alone humans (Mao et al., 2024). Others suggest detectability by design, such as making the building of detection mechanisms into generative AI tools a prerequisite to their release so that users can query content items they are doubtful about (see, notably, Knott et al., 2023). Even when creators of generative models are obliged to identify their output as AI-generated, including in machine-readable formats (see, again, Article 52 of the AI Act), this would only create an incentive for those willing to deceive to resort to obfuscation tools designed to either remove such digital watermarks or alter/erase file metadata. Thus, building detection tools is likely to permanently remain an arms race (Heikkilä, 2023; Májovský et al., 2024; see also Meškys et al., 2020). No less importantly, the success of mandatory identification ultimately depends upon the international standardization of transparency norms, which would be difficult to achieve, particularly in the current global political climate. In this context, an alternative solution might be flipping the argument on its head and establishing human rather than AI origin.

6.2   From Geographical to Human Indications

Another way to contribute to incentivising human authors is to draw upon GIs. Usually associated with agricultural produce, GIs may also be seen as 'powerful marketing tools that enable consumers to differentiate between goods and make rational choices about price, quality and product characteristics' while also protecting the producers from copycats and free riders (Kamperman Sanders, 2010, p. 82). In this sense, GIs benefit both producers and consumers while also promoting development in the relevant geographical areas (Calboli, 2015, p. 761). GIs thereby function as a means to reduce the information asymmetry that consumers are typically faced with (Cardoso et al., 2022, p. 716; see also Moschini et al., 2008) to enable them to make better-informed choices (Ay, 2021, p. 524). In particular, GIs rely on an increased willingness of consumers to know where and how the product they consume has originated and to pay a premium for those with reliable provenance (Sciarra & Gellman, 2012, p. 264). For their part, producers also have a keen interest to 'promote their products, and also prevent fakes and counterfeits from reaching the markets' (Sciarra & Gellman, 2012, p. 264), thus also deriving benefits from increased transparency.

Although pioneered in Europe (for the current version, see Regulation No 1151/2012), the idea of GIs acquired global prominence due to their inclusion in the TRIPS agreement. This globalisation has meant that instead of being merely about the protection of European produce against international competition, as it is still sometimes claimed, GIs are currently used to protect products around the world (Calboli, 2021, p. 290). Notably, GIs are also an important means of protection in cases where other types of intellectual property rights (IPRs) have failed, including in terms of protecting cultural expressions (Rangnekar, 2010, p. 78). This follows the broader trend of reframing culture as a resource because of the deep embeddedness of the economy in broader cultural contexts and institutions (Dagne, 2015, pp. 687–688). Particularly in this context, GIs are fundamentally based on reputation, quality, or similar characteristics associated with a particular geographical area and local traditions (Calboli, 2006, p. 184; Kireeva & O'Connor, 2010, pp. 275–276; Gangjee, 2017a). GIs thus add economic potency to these regional and cultural specificities due to their ability to create scarcity in the market and generate a sense of premium value in the mind of the consumer. As indicated by Calboli (2015, p. 767), GIs allow producers to capture and benefit from 'the value that consumers . . . place on these GI-denominated products', namely, the value added by the perception that the product in question is superior courtesy of its origin (see also Ibele, 2009, pp. 37–38). As argued in the following, it is feasible that the way in which GIs help uphold the value of clearly geographically and culturally defined products in the face of generic competition, indications that affirm human creation, could contribute to the maintenance of the value of artworks in the face of AI-generated competition.

Broadly, GIs function as 'institutional constructions' that connect 'the specific quality and reputation' of the object in question to a given territory (Belletti et al., 2017, p. 45). Quality is specifically attributable to 'the interaction between people and natural resources in a certain territory' (Cardoso et al., 2022, p. 707). GI certification both signals and verifies the qualities and provenance associated with a product that are seen as meriting recognition and protection (Gangjee, 2017b, p. 12) by tracing the origin not only of the end product but also of the ingredients that are used (Sciarra & Gellman, 2012, p. 266). There is, consequently, a dual aim of ensuring 'not only that the interests of the producers concerned are safeguarded against unfair competition, but also that consumers are protected against information which may mislead them' (Gangjee, 2017b, p. 14, original emphasis removed; see also Crescenzi et al., 2022). In this sense, 'food fraud' – misleading labelling that, although not necessarily misappropriating the protected designation, creates the impression that a project originates from the coveted area (such as the use of flags and/or regional symbols on the packaging) – becomes a major issue and is associated with significant economic losses to the local producers (Carreño & Vergano, 2016). Paradoxically, such fraud might be seen as a direct outcome of a GI products' success – when there is more demand for a protected product, there is more incentive for food fraud (Carreño & Vergano, 2016). Here, one can find clear parallels with the attempts to misrepresent AI-generated output as human-created works, although digital items face even more fundamental traceability issues and are certainly not constricted to labelling requirements as strict as those for food products. Therefore, it already becomes evident that neither GIs nor their human equivalents can be seen as magical silver bullets.

Nevertheless, the economic effects that GIs bring are clearly pronounced. Crucially, '[i]n addition to . . . consumer and producer protection, GI protection supports territorial and rural development, biodiversity and traditional knowledge' (Marie-Vivien et al., 2019, p. 2996; see also Calboli, 2021). This is yet again conditioned upon the ability of GIs to generate additional value. Across different domains, empirical studies have demonstrated a general tendency towards 'positive price premium for positively labelled products' (Ay, 2021). In Europe, there is evidence of consumer willingness to prioritise (including paying a premium for) goods that are protected by GIs, thereby indicating the effectiveness of the signalling function typically considered as the cornerstone of this mode of protection (Gangjee, 2017b, p. 15). Notably, the consumer signalling and market limiting functions of GIs can, according to some models, contribute to the production of more high-quality goods than would otherwise be available in the market: since such goods are expensive to produce but demand is uncertain, under normal conditions, underproduction would prevail; however, due to shielding producers from external competition and incentivising consumers to pay a premium, GIs make it rational for producers to invest in quality (Moschini et al., 2008). On the human provenance side, the presence of certification schemes allowing for premium pricing would create incentives for human creativity (on par with manufacturing more artisan, high-quality produce) as opposed to resorting to hybrid or AI-only modes of content production solely geared towards keeping up with the competition.

Crucially, GIs are about taking one aspect of a product and making it absolute as an exclusive source of quality and value. This is, of course, not unprecedented – trademark protection and branding are also premised upon establishing a particular aspect (in this case – symbolic value) as a unique quality symbol. Regarding GIs, meanwhile, denominated products rest on the absolutisation of territory as they are 'said to have unusual, even unique qualities that the place alone can provide' (Raustiala & Munzer, 2007, p. 344; see also Marie-Vivien et al., 2019, p. 2996). As for certifications of human origin, such schemes would also rest on the absolutisation of one particular quality – in this case, on a work having been created by a human. Consequently, in practical terms, GIs are underscored to function (also in the eyes of producers themselves) not so much as marketing tools but as a mechanism for raising entry barriers and thus protecting producer interests (Teuber, 2011, pp. 904–905; see also Marie-Vivien et al., 2019, p. 2996; Crescenzi et al., 2022).

Notably, GIs also have the potential to promote internal solidarity and collective action due to the club nature of such indications (Teuber, 2011, p. 904). Unlike, for example, trademarks that are considered individual property and signal within-industry distinction, GIs are group goods that are collectively established and maintained (Nizam & Tatari, 2022). Also unlike other protection schemes and certifications, community-based rule-building is at the heart of GIs; this, however, pertains to the GIs' nature: '[a]s GIs protect the reputation of a product based on the particular skills and know-how of a local community in a particular geographical area, such local communities are entitled to build their own rules' (Marie-Vivien et al., 2019, p. 2996). It is local actors who prepare the code of practice on which the product's indication is based and are responsible for ensuring adherence (Crescenzi et al., 2022). As such, the argument goes, 'GIs reflect a can-do spirit, with product quality being elaborated, managed and guaranteed by the producers themselves' largely without national or transnational rule-making; therefore, for some at least, GIs represent a grassroots, democratic form of rule-making even though, admittedly, the situation on the ground is not always fair and egalitarian (Marie-Vivien et al., 2019, pp. 2996, 3007).

Indeed, the grassroots-focused story is not *universally* correct – in some cases, when control over a protected indication is limited to a few well-organised actors or dominated by the state, less influential traditional producers may be pushed out of the market (see, e.g., Coombe et al., 2014). Moreover, bureaucracy can still sometimes be an issue that discourages some potential applicants from pursuing GI protection (Quiñones-Ruiz et al., 2016, p. 181). Likewise, although self-organisation is often desirable, it might not always be sufficient protection against low-quality output and free-riding: after all, producers not only are effectively bound to police themselves but also may lack the resources and the knowledge to identify and address infringements – that is, effective governance structures could be an issue (Cardoso et al., 2022, p. 716; see also Nizam & Tatari, 2022, p. 153). Achievement of actual viable protection might be a particularly steep task for smaller groups with limited resources (Giovanucci et al., 2010). However, the shared interests of producers benefitting from a GI can lead to better collaboration and, therefore, trust, which, in turn, encourages information sharing and more efficient GI internal quality assurance (Quiñones-Ruiz et al., 2016, p. 188), although this is also not a uniform tendency. In particular, the impact of cultural and historical factors is felt, such as whether GIs are seen as communal property and, therefore, as a matter of shared interest or as an exploitable resource, open for internal competition (Castelló et al., 2023). In this sense, GIs are fundamentally tied to a specific territory, and their effects can be strongly territorially specific (Cardoso et al., 2022, p. 717).

Continuing on the territorial theme, GIs are seen to partake in a two-tier global competition that is represented by large businesses, supermarket chains, etc. and characterised by uniformity and anonymous supply, on the one hand, and a plethora of more artisanal producers who know their product and supply chain inside out and are thus able to offer unique and locally identifiable goods, on the other hand (Nizam & Tatari, 2022, p. 145). An analogy can be drawn here with competition between AI mass-generated content and artisanal human works. Thus, a suggestion could be made for HIs, that is, certifications of human authorship of artistic or creative works. If, as is likely to happen, the arts market will soon be flooded with inexpensive (or entirely free) AI-generated works, then the fact of human origin could convey added value in the eyes of the consumer (as some of the research cited earlier tentatively indicates). However, without a robust certification procedure, there would be every incentive to pass fully or partly AI-generated works as possessing a 'human touch'; this implies the need to protect authors and provide adequate information to consumers to make informed choices, very similarly to the role ordinarily performed by GIs. In this sense, HIs could allow human artists to capture the additional monetary value inherent in audience perceptions.

As Ferrari (2014) claims, GIs also simultaneously build or contribute to a communal identity that is defined, consolidated, and disseminated to the world outside. Something similar would likely pertain to HIs, especially if communal certification becomes the norm. In this case, both uniting around certain ideas and/or aesthetics and using them as a means of artistic identity expression would coincide and simultaneously contribute to the distinctiveness of HIs. At the same time, horizontal power and verification (effectively, peer responsibility) can be seen as one of the strengths of GI schemes, which ensures that communities have a meaningful say and even control over their traditions. When transposed to the creative domain, the question of the appropriate level of HI certification arises: whether there should be a global set of regulations, national/regional ones, or perhaps, certification should be managed by artists' collectives. Building on the grassroots, self-efficiency expanding nature of GI certification, it is foreseeable that HI certification could be carried out by artists' collectives and similar groups congregated around a shared aesthetic, worldview/ideological, tool/method, or any other preference. Of course, the drawback of such decentralised certification would be the unequal robustness of standards and internal control. However, it is important to keep in mind that, despite the often community-centric nature of GIs, an important role is still played by the state, such as in the creation of legal frameworks, enforcement, and pursuit of GI owners' interests abroad (Marie-Vivien & Biénabe, 2017). The latter becomes much more problematic given the largely deterritorialised nature of HIs since it would be unclear which, if any, states or regional organisations would ultimately have the jurisdiction over particular HIs. However, if states *do* get involved, this would still not preclude the emergence of divergent (this time, national or regional) standards that could lead to unequal opportunities for human creators in a global digital marketplace. A truly global regime would ensure a uniformity of rules, thus harmonising producer and consumer expectations and leading to more efficient enforcement (particularly in terms of international trade), but it would be significantly more cumbersome. Thus, the introduction of HIs would face similar challenges arising from the mismatch between the territorial nature of traditional governance and the borderless nature of the digital environment, which most issues of technology regulation face.

There are nevertheless also benefits to a lack of territorial focus in HIs. Notably, GIs are ill-equipped to deal with some of the fundamental challenges underpinning today's world, perhaps most notably, climate change. As climatic conditions shift and the original *terroir* becomes no longer viable for the protected product (or the traditional means of production), the relocation of production or major changes to production methods are precluded by the very nature of GIs (see, e.g., Borghini et al., 2023; Henry, 2023). However, the deterritorialised nature of HIs would preclude such challenges. Moreover, there is often criticism of GIs being geared towards protecting goods of European origin against the rest of the world, while perhaps no such controversy would exist regarding GIs – except for, that is, the debate as to whether humans deserve special protection in the first place, with criticisms potentially coming from both market-centric and value-centric (critical or posthumanist) approaches. The crux of the matter here is that at least as long as certification is open to authors of any background (such as whether certification is carried out by organically congregated authors' collectives), no particular group would likely get special preference.

However, certain problems persist. As shown in the previous section, the actual level of value premium and the size of the market for more expensive HI-certified works are, as yet, indeterminate. Moreover, although the verification process of the origin of agricultural produce is relatively straightforward, for HIs, due to the intangibility of digital tools, the verification of human origin (or a certain percentage of human involvement) would likely be significantly more complicated. Likewise, if effective governance structures and the elimination of free-riding can be an issue even when it comes to the oversight of highly territorial GI claims (see, e.g., Nizam & Tatari, 2022), then the protection of HIs online is likely to be even more complicated. Furthermore, even in territory-focused GIs, it is difficult to ascertain who is entitled to use the indication and who is not – which at the very least, incurs significant administrative costs (see, e.g., Montén, 2006). In the case of generative AI, this not only involves dealing with significantly more amorphous and vaguely inter-connected communities but also potentially implies the need for highly reliable detection tools.

There are also notable discussions around GIs and innovation: some interpret the protectionist nature of GIs and their focus on tradition as innovation-stifling, while others put more emphasis on how innovation takes place *within* the protected tradition (for a discussion, see Stranieri et al., 2023). In either case, truly paradigm-shifting innovation is likely to be out of the question. Likewise, the collectivist nature of HI certification might also stifle the adoption of novel styles, techniques, and particularly, tools. In this case, the grassroots collective-focused mode of certification would likely prove to be the most conservative. A related criticism includes the possibility of protected traditional and place-focused ways of manufacturing, which threaten to 'block private initiative and create useless or ineffective . . . products' (Belletti et al., 2017, p. 55). The argument thus goes that products unable to withstand competition should probably not be produced in the first place, just like competitiveness-reducing production methods should be confined to history. In this way, the protection of culture, tradition, and heritage is seen by critics of GIs as merely convenient distractions from what they consider to be the main aim of such protection – the distortion of competition and international trade, that is, a reincarnation of mercantilist protectionism in a global system otherwise committed to the progressive realisation of free trade under frameworks such as the World Trade Organisation (see, e.g., Broude, 2005; Raustiala & Munzer, 2007). However, it could be counter-argued that HIs would have no such market-distorting effects: in terms of GIs, the protection of a particular type of produce automatically fences it off for other producers, whereas artistic creativity is premised upon fixing a particular expression of ideas onto a medium. Hence, the labelling of a particular fixed expression of an idea as human-created does not in any way limit the ability of others to create or generate alternative unlabelled expressions.

Overall, then, the establishment of HIs constitutes a potentially viable way of incentivising human creativity, albeit one that is still, similar to others discussed in this book, not without its pitfalls and drawbacks. It is certainly unlikely to provide *the* magic solution to preserving author remuneration in the context of generative AI. However, it could be considered one of the potential policy options, possibly in combination with some of the others. At the very least, HIs would likely contribute to solving information asymmetries in the art market by providing indications (even if not always fully reliable) as to the origin of the work in question, thus benefitting not only artists but also consumers.

Bibliography

Arango, L., Singaraju, S. P., & Niininen, O. (2023). Consumer responses to AI-generated charitable giving ads. *Journal of Advertising, 52*(4), 486–503.

Audry, S., & Ippolito, J. (2019). Can artificial intelligence make arti without artists? Ask the viewer. *Arts, 8*(1), 1–8.

Ay, J.-S. (2021). The Informational Content of Geographical Indications. *American Journal of Agricultural Economics, 103*(2), 523–542.

BaHammam, A. S. (2023). Balancing innovation and integrity: The role of AI in research and scientific writing. *Nature and Science of Sleep, 15*, 1153–11.

Banh, L., & Strobel, G. (2023). Generative artificial intelligence. *Electronic Markets, 33*, 1–17.

Belletti, G., Marescotti, A., & Touzard, J.-M. (2017). Geographical indications, public goods, and sustainable development: The roles of actors' strategies and public policies. *World Development, 98*, 45–57.

Borghini, A., Piras, N., & Serini, B. (2023). Hot grapes: How to locally redesign geographical indications to address the impact of climate change. *World Development Sustainability, 2,* 1–9.

Bown, O. (2021). *Beyond the creative species: Making machines that make art and music.* The MIT Press.

Broude, T. (2005). Taking trade and culture seriously: Geographical indications and cultural protection in WTO law. *University of Pennsylvania Journal of International Economic Law, 26*(4), 623–692.

Calboli, I. (2006). Expanding the protection of geographical indications of origin under TRIPS: 'Old' debate or 'new' opportunity. *Marquette Intellectual Property Law Review, 10*(2), 181–203.

Calboli, I. (2015). Geographical indications of origin at the crossroads of local development, consumer protection and marketing strategies. *IIC – In46ternational Review of Intellectual Property and Competition Law, 46,* 760–780.

Calboli, I. (2021). Geographical indications: New perspectives and recent developments. *Journal of Intellectual Property Law & Practice, 16*(4–5), 289–290.

Cardoso, V. A., et al. (2022). The benefits and barriers of geographical indications to producers: A review. *Renewable Agriculture and Food Systems, 37*(6), 707–719.

Carreño, I., & Vergano, P. R. (2016). Geographical indications, 'food fraud' and the fight against 'Italian sounding' products. *European Journal of Risk Regulation, 7*(2), 416–420.

Castelló, E., Lövgren, D., & Svensson, G. (2023). The narratives of geographical indications as commons: A study of Catalan and Swedish cases. *Food, Culture & Society: An International Journal of Multidisciplinary Research, 26*(5), 1014–1031.

Chung, J. (2023). AI luddites: Consumers penalize creative work output generated by artificial intelligence. *Research Square.* https://doi.org/10.21203/rs.3.rs-3444321/v1.

Cohen, J. E. (2007). Creativity and culture in copyright theory. *University of California Davis Law Review, 40,* 1151–1205.

Coombe, R. J., Ives, S., & Huizenga, D. (2014). Geographical indications: The promise, perils and politics of protecting place-based products. In M. David & D. Halbert (Eds.), *SAGE handbook on intellectual property* (pp. 224–237). SAGE Publications.

Crescenzi, R., et al. (2022). Geographical indications and local development: The strength of territorial embeddedness. *Regional Studies, 56*(3), 381–393.

Dagne, T. W. (2015). Beyond economic considerations: (Re)Conceptualizing geographical indications for protecting traditional agricultural products. *IIC – In46ternational Review of Intellectual Property and Competition Law, 46,* 682–706.

De Cremer, D., Bianzino, N. M., & Falk, B. (2023, April 13). How generative AI could disrupt creative work. *Harvard Business Review.* https://hbr.org/2023/04/how-generative-ai-could-disrupt-creative-work.

Epstein, Z., et al. (2020). Who gets credit for AI-generated art? *iScience, 23,* 1–16.

Ferrari, M. (2014). The narratives of geographical indications. *International Journal of Law in Context, 10*(2), 222–248.

Fortuna, P., & Modliński, A. (2021). A(I)rtist or counterfeiter? Artificial intelligence as (D)Evaluating factor on the AI art market. *The Journal of Arts Management, Law, and Society, 51*(3), 188–201.

Gangadharbatla, H. (2022). The role of AI attribution knowledge in the evaluation of artwork. *Empirical Studies of the Arts, 40*(2), 125–145.

Gangjee, D. S. (2017a). From geography to history: Geographical indications and the reputational link. In I. Calboli & W. L. Ng-Loy (Eds.), *Geographical indications at the crossroads of trade, development, and culture in the Asia-Pacific* (pp. 36–60). Cambridge University Press.

Gangjee, D. S. (2017b). Proving provenance? Geographical indications certification and its ambiguities. *World Development, 98,* 12–24.

Giovanucci, D., Barham, E., & Pirog, R. (2010). Defining and marketing 'local' foods: Geographical indications for US products. *The Journal of World Intellectual Property, 13*(2), 94–120.

Heikkilä, M. (2023, February 7). Why detecting AI-generated text is so difficult (and What to Do About It). *MIT Technology Review.* www.technologyreview.com/2023/02/07/1067928/why-detecting-ai-generated-text-is-so-difficult-and-what-to-do-about-it/.

Henry, L. (2023). Adapting the designated area of geographical indications to climate change. *American Journal of Agricultural Economics, 105,* 1088–1115.

Hitsuwari, J., Ueda, Y., Yun, W., & Nomura, M. (2023). Does human-AI collaboration lead to more creative art? Aesthetic evaluation of human-made and AI-generated haiku poetry. *Computers in Human Behavior, 139,* 1–10.

Hodges, C. B., & Kirschner, P. A. (2024). Innovation of instructional design and assessment in the age of generative artificial intelligence. *TechTrends, 68,* 195–199.

Hoel, E. (2021, September 8). Big tech is replacing human artists with AI. *The Intrinsic Perspective.* https://erikhoel.substack.com/p/big-tech-is-replacing-human-artists.

Hong, J.-W., & Curran, N. M. (2019). Artificial intelligence, artists, and art: Attitudes towards artwork produced by humans vs. Artificial intelligence. *ACM Transactions on Multimedia Computing, Communications, and Applications, 15*(2), 1–6.

Hong, J.-W., Peng, Q., & Williams, D. (2021). Are you ready for artificial mozart and skrillex? An experiment testing expectancy violation theory and AI music. *New Media & Society, 23*(7), 1290–1935.

Ibele, E. W. (2009). The nature and function of geographical indications in law. *The Estey Centre Journal of International Law and Trade Policy, 10*(1), 36–49.

Kamperman Sanders, A. (2010). Incentives for and protection of cultural expression: Art, trade and geographical indications. *Journal of World Intellectual Property, 13*(2), 81–93.

Kireeva, I., & O'Connor, B. (2010). Geographical Indications and the TRIPS agreement: What protection is provided to geographical indications in WTO members. *Journal of World Intellectual Property, 13*(2), 275–303.

Knott, A., Pedreschi, D., Chatila, R., Chakraborti, T., Leavy, S., Baeza-Yates, R., Eyers, D., Trotman, A., Teal, P. D., Biecek, P., Russell, S., & Bengio, Y. (2023). Generative AI models should include detection mechanisms as a condition for public release. *Ethics and Information Technology, 25*, 1–7.

Köbis, N., & Mossink, L. D. (2021). Artificial intelligence versus Maya Angelou: Experimental evidence that people cannot differentiate AI-generated from human-written poetry. *Computers in Human Behavior, 114*, 1–13.

Kostygina, G., Kim, Y., Seeskin, Z., LeClere, F., & Emery, S. (2023). Disclosure standards for social media and generative artificial intelligence research: Toward transparency and replicability. *Social Media + Society.* https://doi.org/10.1177/20563051231216947.

Májovský, M., Černý, M., Netuka, D., & Mikolov, T. (2024). Perfect detection of computer-generated text faces fundamental challenges. *Cell Reports Physical Science, 5*, 1–5.

Makhortykh, M., Zucker, E. M., Simon, D. J., Bultmann, D., & Ulloa, R. (2023). Shall androids dream of genocides? How generative AI can change the future of memorialization of mass atrocities. *Discover Artificial Intelligence, 3*, 1–17.

Mao, J., Chen, B., & Liu, C. (2024). Generative artificial intelligence in education and its implications for assessment. *TechTrends, 68*, 58–66.

Marie-Vivien, D., & Biénabe, E. (2017). The multifaceted role of the state in the protection of geographical indications: A worldwide review. *World Development, 98*, 1–11.

Marie-Vivien, D., Carimentrand, A., Fournier, S., Cerdan, C., & Sautier, D. (2019). Controversies around geographical indications: Are democracy and representativeness the solution? *British Food Journal, 121*(12), 2995–3010.

Mazzone, M., & Elgammal, A. (2019). Art, creativity, and the potential of artificial intelligence. *Arts, 8*(1), 1–9.

Meškys, E., Liaudanskas, A., Kalpokiene, J., & Jurcys, P. (2020). Regulating deep fakes: Legal and ethical considerations. *Journal of Intellectual Property Law & Practice, 15*(1), 24–31.

Messingschlager, T. V., & Appel, M. (2023). Mind ascribed to ai and the appreciation of AI-generated art. *New Media & Society.* https://doi.org/10.1177/14614448231200248.

Mikalonytė, E. S., & Kneer, M. (2022). Can artificial intelligence make art? Folk intuitions as to whether AI-driven robots can be viewed as artists and produce art. *ACM Transactions on Human-Robot Interaction, 11*(4), 1–19.

Millet, K., Buehler, F., Du, G., & Kokkoris, M. D. (2023). Defending humankind: Anthropocentric bias in the appreciation of AI art. *Computers in Human Behavior, 143*, 1–9.

Montén, L. (2006). Geographical indications of origin: Should they be protected and why? – An analysis of the issue from the US and EU perspectives. *Santa Clara Computer and High Technology Law Journal, 22*, 315–349.

Moschini, G., Menapace, L., & Pick, D. (2008). Geographical indications and the competitive provision of quality in agricultural markets. *American Journal of Agricultural Economics, 90*(3), 794–812.

Moura, F. T., & Maw, C. (2021). Artificial intelligence became beethoven: How do listeners and music professionals perceive artificially composed music? *Journal of Consumer Marketing, 38*(2), 137–146.

Nah, F. F. H., Zheng, R., Cai, J., Siau, K., & Chen, L. (2023). Generative AI and ChatGPT: Applications, challenges, and AI-human collaboration. *Journal of Information Technology Case and Application Research, 25*(3), 277–304.

Nizam, D., & Tatari, M. F. (2022). Rural revitalization through territorial distinctiveness: The use of geographical indications in Turkey. *Journal of Rural Studies, 93*, 144–154.

Ooi, K. B., Wei-Han Tan G., Al-Emran, M., Al-Sharafi, M. A., Capatina, A., Chakraborty, A., Dwivedi, Y. K., Huang, T. L., Kar A. K., Lee V. H., Loh, X. M., Micu, A., Mikalef, P., Mogaji, E., Pandey, N., Raman, R., Rana N. P., Sarker, P., Sharma, A., Teng, C., Wamba, S. F., & Wong, L. W. (2023). The potential of generative artificial intelligence across disciplines: Perspectives and future directions. *Journal of Computer Information Systems.* https://doi.org/10.1080/08874417.2023.2261010.

Ornes, S. (2019). Computers take art in new directions, challenging the meaning of 'creativity'. *Proceedings of the National Academy of Sciences of the United States of America, 116*(11), 4760–4763.

Park, J., Kang, H., & Kim, H. Y. (2023). Human, do you think this painting is the work of a real artist? *International Journal of Human-Computer Interaction.* https://doi.org/10.1080/10447318.2023.2232978.

Peukert, C. (2019). The next wave of digital technological change and the cultural industries. *Journal of Cultural Economics, 43*, 189–210.

Quiñones-Ruiz, X. F., Penker, M., Belletti, G., Marescotti, A., & Scaramuzzi, S. (2016). Why early collective action pays off: Evidence from setting protecting geographical indications. *Renewable Agriculture and Food Systems, 32*(2), 179–192.

Rangnekar, D. (2010). The law and economics of geographical indications. *Journal of World Intellectual Property, 13*(2), 77–80.

Raustiala, K., & Munzer, S. R. (2007). The global struggle over geographic indications. *The European Journal of International Law, 18*(2), 337–365.

Sciarra, A. F., & Gellman, L. (2012). Geographical indications: Why traceability systems matter and how they add to brand value. *Journal of Intellectual Property Law & Practice, 7*(4), 264–270.

Senftleben, M. (2023). Generative AI and author remuneration. *IIC – International Review of Intellectual Property and Competition Law, 54*, 1535–1560.

Stranieri, S. et al. (2023). Geographical Indications and Innovation: Evidence from EU Regions. *Food Policy, 116*, 1–15.

Sun, D., Wang, H., & Xiong, J. (2023). Would you like to listen to my music, my friend? An experiment on AI musicians. *International Journal of Human-Computer Interaction.* https://doi.org/10.1080/10447318.2023.2181872.

Tang, A., Li, K. K., Kwok, K. O., Cao, L., Luong, S., & Tam, W. (2023). The importance of transparency: Declaring the use of generative Artificial Intelligence (AI) in academic writing. *Journal of Nursing Scholarship.* https://doi.org/10.1111/jnu.12938.

Teuber, R. (2011). Consumers' and producers' expectations towards geographical indications: Empirical evidence for a German case study. *British Food Journal, 113*(7), 900–918.

Tigre Moura, F. and Maw, C. (2021). Artificial Intelligence Became Beethoven: How do Listeners and Music Professionals Perceive Artificially Composed Music? *Journal of Consumer Marketing, 38*(2), 137–146.

Tigre Moura, F., Castrucci, C., & Hindley, C. (2023). Artificial intelligence creates art? An experimental investigation of value and creativity perceptions. *Journal of Creative Behavior.* https://doi.org/10.1002/jocb.600.

Tubadji, A. Huang, H., & Webber, D. J. (2021). Cultural proximity bias in AI-acceptability: The importance of being human. *Technological Forecasting & Social Change, 173,* 1–14.

Veale, T., & Pérez y Pérez, R. (2020). Leaps and bounds: An introduction to the field of computational creativity. *New Generation Computing, 38,* 551–563.

Velthuis, O. (2013). Art markets. In R. Towse (Ed.), *A handbook of cultural economics* (2nd ed., pp. 33–42). Edward Elgar.

Williams, R. T. (2024). The ethical implications of using generative chatbots in higher education. *Frontiers in Education, 8,* 1–8.

Wingström, R., Hautala, J., & Lundman, R. (2022). Redefining creativity in the era of AI? Perspectives of computer scientists and new media artists. *Creativity Research Journal.* https://doi.org/10.1080/10400419.2022.2107850.

Treaties and Legislation

International

Agreement on Trade-related Aspects of Intellectual Property Rights (TRIPS) (1869 U.N.T.S. 299).

European Union

Proposal for a Regulation of the European Parliament and of the Council Laying Down Harmonised Rules on Artificial Intelligence (Artificial Intelligence Act) and Amending Certain Union Legislative Acts, COM/2021/206 final.

Regulation (EU) No 1151/2012 of the European Parliament and of the Council of 21 November 2012 on Quality Schemes for Agricultural Products and Foodstuffs.

7   Conclusion

As argued in this book, the advent of generative AI is likely to have an impact on the economic standing of human authors and their incentives to create. Even more importantly, however, such effects are not easily manageable or ameliorated. Certainly, it must be admitted that neither the meaning of creativity nor the status of the human author has been stable over time and across cultures. Likewise, following Navas (2023, p. 3), '[a]s artificial intelligence continues to develop, creativity continues to be redefined beyond humanistic presumptions'. The necessary interplay among individual-level internal motivations, cultural and contextual influences, and extrinsic motivations in creativity (see generally Cohen, 2007) implies a malleability of what counts as art and artist, preventing an overly rigid fixation of the status quo. This is particularly relevant given the tendencies, identified early on in this book, for any present system to establish and maintain oversimplified dichotomies and hierarchies that normalise existing patterns of domination and discrimination in line with the dominant ideological and economic interests of the day. In light of this, there is a two-fold threat: on the one hand, as previously discussed, overly exclusionary notions of creativity, instead of preserving human creativity *as such*, end up protecting only a subset of humanity and economically dominant actors; on the other hand, there is also a threat that by stretching the notion of creativity and protection or alternative monetisation opportunities to technology-enabled actors, one would only end up serving the economic and cultural interests of the new socio-political hierarchies, this time dominated not by gendered or racialised elites but by large technology companies, again at the expense of human authors (or the majority thereof).

It must be emphasised that generative AI and its association with creativity (or processes resembling it) is symptomatic of the day and age. After all, we live in 'a world of data, in which much communication is controlled by powerful algorithms' to the extent that '[a]lgorithms make the world go round' (Potts, 2023, pp. 4, 135). Therefore, it might seem only natural that under such conditions also '[p]art of current cultural value is produced by machine learning algorithms for the consumption of humans' (Navas, 2023, p. 189). As the very figure of the author becomes destabilised by way of generative AI

DOI: 10.4324/9781003464976-7

irrupting into the domain of creativity, the straightforward replacement of a (unitary) human author with a (unitary) machine author is not possible either. This, in turn, manifests 'serious critical implications not only for the aesthetic interpretation of AI art, but also for socio-economic perspectives on originality, the AI art author figure, and the legal status of the AI artwork itself' (Zeilinger, 2021, p. 162). A somewhat similar argument is also presented by Fenwick and Jurcys (2023, p. 3) who assert that 'there is no such thing as a purely AI-generated work': after all, at least as of now and in the foreseeable future, humans remain involved in the concept formulation, prompting, refinement, and deployment of such content. A focus on the 'AI-generated' aspect of such content would, for these authors, be 'overly simplistic and potentially misleading' (Fenwick & Jurcys, 2023, p. 11). The focus of Navas (2023, p. 250), meanwhile, is not on overcoming the attribution of creativity or authorship to any of the summands but instead focusing on 'the creative process itself'. Nevertheless, regardless of the framing, a reduction in incentives to human authors is a likely outcome and one that, as shown throughout the book, does not lend itself to simplistic solutions.

Generative AI should definitely not be vilified. To begin with, it provides avenues for creative self-expression to a much broader subset of humanity, including those who would have otherwise lacked the skills, knowledge, and aptitude to engage in creative endeavours. Moreover, generative AI could break down the ableist understanding of art by making creative expression available to everyone regardless of their neuro-physical characteristics (Newton & Dhole, 2023). In adopting a broader perspective, generative AI can also be seen as challenging discriminatory anthropocentrism in aesthetics, which is understood as 'a discourse of engagement with the world that the human subject projects onto nature as an "other" to be territorialized' (Navas, 2023, p. 245). Nevertheless, negative consequences are also not mere speculations but are already beginning to emerge. For example, one can already witness signs of the inundation of creative spaces with AI-generated output (Nover, 2023), with the risk of human artists simply being crowded out or their works becoming lost within the flood of AI-generated content (Hoover, 2023). Moreover, despite initiatives to either thwart the web crawling processes that feed learning models (see, e.g., Knibbs, 2023a) or watermark AI-generated output (see, e.g., Knibbs, 2023b), such initiatives remain embroiled in a technology race between generation and thwarting/detection.

Another issue to consider entails the problematic assumption of technological agency continuing in a straight, predefined line. As Howcroft and Taylor (2023, p. 365) observe, there is a 'lacuna of agency' in the current highly deterministic discourse of technological change, with the focus being on its alleged objective linear unavoidability. In this vein, there is an argument to be made that adjustments in societal tastes in response to technological change would lead to a new equilibrium without any need for additional measures, simultaneously also curving the line of technological development. Pelc (2023), for example, refers to the Arts and Crafts movement in nineteenth-century Britain that, as a reaction to the proliferation of standardised factory-made goods, popularised hand-made artisanal alternatives. Similarly, for AI, when it becomes more prevalent, more value will be ascribed to human-created works. Nevertheless, in addition to issues pertaining to verification and proof of origin as discussed in this book, an additional issue is individuals' ability to pay: although there might be a large proportion of the population who prefer artisanal goods, equating preference with affordability is potentially elitist and insensitive to the actual living conditions of individuals. Likewise, if the growing trend towards digital spirituality (see, e.g., Fisher, 2023) is anything to go by, then humans may infer deeper and more hidden meanings into AI's output. More broadly, however, some would laud the revelatory quality of AI models for their 'potential to tell us something new about ourselves' by 'picking up traits in our human code that we still haven't been able to articulate in words' (Du Sautoy, 2020, p. 87). In this vein, as with previous technical progress, it seems that both the human author and AI outputs will coexist, thus changing the status quo for the human author.

Collective action can be a strong tool in asserting the rights of human authors, with the agreement reached between Hollywood writers and film companies to end the 2023 strike standing out as a notable example, particularly in terms of assurances that human writers would not be replaced with generative AI (Bedingfield, 2023). Nevertheless, it must be emphasised that for similar results to be achieved elsewhere, several factors are necessary, such as high levels of unionisation or other forms of coordinating collective action and a clear and narrowly identifiable group of stakeholders to negotiate with. Notably, even the agreement in question is only binding on the film studios and does not prohibit, for example, technology companies training AI scriptwriters (Bedingfield, 2023) and, potentially, even producing films (especially given the growing video generation capacities). Although collective action resulting in similar agreements may contribute to solutions, the effectiveness of such measures is doubtful, particularly in situations where only limited organisation exists, as potential implementors of AI are numerous, and international competition is rife.

Moreover, the enabling resource of generative AI – namely, data – is not without controversies. Indeed, it can be said that the 'flood' of continuously accumulated data has become 'the main catalyst for the new age of machine learning' (Du Sautoy, 2020, p. 67). Nevertheless, the 'flood' analogy is misleading: while a flood is naturally occurring and takes place without (and often even against) human will, data proliferation is the consequence of deliberate actions. In this sense, 'objects and . . . spaces have both become embedded in digital technologies' so that any element of the 'smart' digital whole can no longer operate independently (Käll, 2023, p. 42). As Knight (2023) puts it, not only 'the generative AI boom has made the tech industry . . . even more hungry for data than it already was' but also AI has become perceived as 'a kind of monster that has to be fed at all costs', thereby leaving companies in a constant search for new kinds of data that are either already owned or could potentially be acquired.

A further issue arises at this point: the collection, storage, and analysis of data come at a significant environmental cost in terms of resources for hardware manufacturing and the continuous demand for electricity and cooling to keep the systems running; moreover, such environmental costs not only pertain to the data collection and training stages of generative AI but also increase with every deployment of the tools in question by any end user (see, e.g., Gordon et al., 2023; Heikkilä, 2023). For this reason, the idea of AI-generated content being cheap only holds as long as the price of resources, such as electricity and water, continues to fail to reflect the actual harms caused. Factoring in the true costs might make AI-generated content less attractive and give some more breathing space to human authors. Nevertheless, price inflation across the economy would also simultaneously dilute the value of any financial incentives for human authors.

Several additional problematic aspects become relevant in this context. First is the unlocking of latent value in works-as-data that pertains to learning not only artistic styles but also the contextual information about the world that has to come from somebody's input. For this reason, some would assert that already, 'the story of the Web is labor theft' (Merkley, 2023). Secondly, data pertain not only to content but also to its perception. In this sense, it seems plausible that AI could substitute human authors by learning to satisfy audience needs for a fraction of the cost. Arguably, this has contributed to AI-generated outputs being banned from some online fora and stock image platforms (see, e.g., Edwards, 2022; Vincent, 2022). In light of the arguments presented in this book, licencing schemes or guaranteed author income modelled after UBI could be partial solutions to remuneration issues, whereas CSR/CDR initiatives may slow the pace of human substitution.

Contrary to, for example, Tredinnick and Laybats (2023), foresight and threat mitigation rather than immediate embrace should characterise our relationship with new and emerging technologies. After all, it must be kept in mind that even within the digital domain, 'knowledge and information never flow freely but always depend on various matters of mediation' (Käll, 2023, p. 76), which means that they are also always entangled with the dominant societal and economic practices, which can often be exclusionary and even discriminative. Also notable in this context is the likely further extension of the digital divide in terms of unequal access to connectivity, hardware, and software (Pappas et al., 2023, p. 947); this includes a lack of equality in access to AI tools, a preclusion of competition in a technology-centric environment, and a lack of access to verification (for both digital tools and collective means, such as HIs). Accordingly, regulatory measures have to be put in place to ensure the protection of the interests of the groups rendered vulnerable by technological change.

Although some (see, e.g., Ashton & Patel, 2024) claim that celebrity robot artists, such as Ai-Da, represent a posthumanisation of authorship through the cultivation of an artistic persona (thus allegedly demonstrating the embeddedness and interrelatedness of artistic creativity), they still serve as a nod to the established idea of the author being the personalisation of creativity: the author is, if not human, then at least human*oid*. Just like the figure of the romantic heroic author distracts attention from the actual toil of creative labour, here, the construction of a machinic 'author' distracts attention from 'faceless' disembodied models; likewise, a focus on the novelty and brand value of celebrity robots precludes engagement with the more fundamental background effects of generative AI, namely, its challenge to the livelihoods of an entire class of human authors who not only work individually but also constitute the labour force of the creative industries. As shown in this book, copyright, in its current or revised form, is not going to have a substantial effect in improving the plight of human authors. Instead, should societies, through their elected representatives, decide to protect human creativity by providing additional incentives, a combination of further means is necessary, including subsidising human authors, encouraging or mandating corporate responsibility practices, and/or introducing systems of proving the human origin of works. As already indicated, none of these solutions is without fault, and consequently, there cannot be a silver bullet to solve the challenges faced by human authors. Nevertheless, these approaches can still function as parts of a more complex set of solutions.

Bibliography

Ashton, D., & Patel, K. (2024). 'People don't buy art, they buy artists: Robot artists – Work, identity, and expertise. *Convergence: The International Journal of Research into New Media Technologies.* https://doi.org/10.1177/13548565231220310.

Bedingfield, W. (2023, September 27). Hollywood writers reached an AI deal that will rewrite history. *Wired.* www.wired.COM/story/us-writers-strike-ai-provisions-precedents/.

Cohen, J. E. (2007). Creativity and culture in copyright theory. *University of California Davis Law Review, 40,* 1151–1205.

Du Sautoy, M. (2020). *The creativity code: How AI is learning to write, paint and think.* 4th Estate.

Edwards, B. (2022, September 12). Flooded with AI-generated images, some art communities ban them completely. *Ars Technica.* https://arstechnica.com/information-technology/2022/09/flooded-with-ai-generated-images-some-art-communities-ban-them-completely/.

Fenwick, M., & Jurcys, P. (2023). Originality and the future of copyright in an age of generative AI. *Computer Law & Security Review: The International Journal of Technology Law and Practice, 51,* 1–12.

Fisher, N. S. (2023, October 5). Generative AI has ushered in the next phase of digital spirituality. *Wired.* www.wired.com/story/artificial-intelligence-spirituality-tarot/.

Gordon, A., Jafari, A., & Higgs, C. (2023, July 19). The hidden cost of the AI boom: Social and environmental exploitation. *The Conversation*. https://theconversation.com/the-hidden-cost-of-the-ai-boom-social-and-environmental-exploitation-208669.

Grimmelmann, J. (2016). Copyright for literate robots. *Iowa Law Review*, *101*(2), 657–682.

Heikkilä, M. (2023, December 1). Making an image with generative AI uses as much energy as charging your phone. *The MIT Technology Review*. www.technologyreview.com/2023/12/01/1084189/making-an-image-with-generative-ai-uses-as-much-energy-as-charging-your-phone/.

Hoover, A. (2023, April 17). AI-generated music is about to flood streaming platforms. *Wired*. www.wired.com/story/ai-generated-music-streaming-services-copyright/.

Howcroft, D., & Taylor, P. (2023). Automation and the future of work: A social shaping of technology approach. *New Technology, Work and Employment*, *38*, 351–370.

Käll, J. (2023). *Posthuman property and law: Commodification and control through information, smart spaces and artificial intelligence*. Routledge.

Knibbs, K. (2023a, October 12). A new tool helps artists thwart AI – With a middle finger. *Wired*. www.wired.com/story/kudurru-ai-scraping-block-poisoning-spawning/.

Knibbs, K. (2023b, October 3). Researchers tested AI watermarks – And broke all of them. *Wired*. www.wired.com/story/artificial-intelligence-watermarking-issues/.

Knight, W. (2023, August 10). Generative AI is making companies even more thirsty for your data. *Wired*. www.wired.com/story/fast-forward-generative-ai-companies-thirsty-for-your-data/.

Lim, D. (2018). AI & IP: Innovation creativity in an age of accelerated change. *Akron Law Review*, *52*(3), 813–876.

Merkley, R. (2023, February 27). On AI-generated works, artists, and intellectual property. *Lawfare*. www.lawfaremedia.org/article/ai-generated-works-artists-and-intellectual-property.

Navas, E. (2023). *The rise of metacreativity: AI aesthetics after remix*. Routledge.

Newton, A., & Dhole, K. (2023). Is AI art another industrial revolution in the making? *arXiv*. https://arxiv.org/abs/2301.05133.

Nover, S. (2023, February 22). Sci-Fi magazine has to halt submissions after receiving too much AI-generated fiction. *Quartz*. https://qz.com/clarkesword-neil-clarke-chatgpt-ai-q-and-a-1850144881.

Pappas, I. O., Mikalef, P., Dwivedi, Y. K., Jaccheri, L., & Krogstie, J. (2023). Responsible digital transformation for a sustainable society. *Information Systems Frontiers*, *25*, 245–253.

Pelc, K. (2023, March 16). AI will make human art more valuable. *Wired*. www.wired.com/story/art-artificial-intelligence-history/.

Potts, J. (2023). *The near-death of the author: Creativity in the internet age*. The University of Toronto Press.

Tredinnick, L., & Laybats, C. (2023). The dangers of generative artificial intelligence. *Business Information Review*, *40*(2), 46–48.

Vincent, J. (2022, September 21). Getty images bans AI-generated content over fears of legal challenges. *The Verge.* www.theverge.com/2022/9/21/23364696/ getty-images-ai-ban-generated-artwork-illustration-copyright.

Zeilinger, M. (2021). *Tactical entanglements: AI art, creative agency, and the limits of intellectual property.* Meson Press.

Index

For Product Safety Concerns and Information please contact our EU representative GPSR@taylorandfrancis.com Taylor & Francis Verlag GmbH, Kaufingerstraße 24, 80331 München, Germany

Printed and bound by CPI Group (UK) Ltd, Croydon, CR0 4YY
08/06/2025
01896998-0008